EIGHT LEADERTYPES IN THE WHITE HOUSE

DISCOVER AND LEVERAGE YOUR OVAL OFFICE LEADERSHIP STYLE

BY CASH KEAHEY

Inspire On Purpose Publishing

Irving, Texas

Eight LeaderTypes in the White House:
Discover and Leverage Your Oval Office Leadership Style

Copyright © 2018 Cash Keahey

Inspire On Purpose Publishing
Irving, Texas
(888) 403-2727
https://inspireonpurpose.com
The Platform Publisher™
"Changing Lives With Words"

Printed in the United States of America

Library of Congress Control Number: 2018930068
ISBN-13: 978-1-941782-47-7

For more information about the author and book,
visit: https://leadertype.com

To the memory of Jack Keahey,

my father and first leader.

For Jared and Jillian,

and their generation:

May you lead the world better.

ACKNOWLEDGMENTS

THAT I STAND ON the shoulders of giants is a gross understatement.

Among those who have passed, I am eternally grateful for the teachings of Carl Gustav Jung, and thankful that Isabel Briggs Myers' journey was about making Jung's theory practical and accessible. Otto Kroeger and Janet Thuesen qualified me to administer the Myers-Briggs Type Indicator® (MBTI), shaping my initial understanding of type. I learned a lot about organizational and leadership development from Doug McQueen. I am most grateful for my father, who taught me about leadership through his example. His ideals still shape and motivate me, and his pride in me still gives me confidence. I dedicate this book to the memory of Jack Keahey, a Proactive-Independent leader.

I especially thank Steven J. Rubenzer and Thomas R. Faschingbauer, authors of *Personality, Character and Leadership in the White House,* for getting 120 historian-experts to assess 42 presidents' personality traits, and for allowing me to use their data, without which this book would not have been possible. I thank both men for their groundbreaking research, painstaking analysis and noteworthy results.

Danielle Poirier has been my tireless teacher, helper and supporter for more than 10 years. Her *Magnificent 16* DVD is a multimedia tour-de-force exploration of the sixteen Myers-Briggs types from which I drew many lessons. She specifically helped me define items for my LeaderType™ Indicator, categorize items on the NEO PI-R (See Appendix 1.), and evaluate hundreds of quotes in terms of type preference. She also reviewed my near-final manuscript, and offered essential input on the introverted feeling chapter, among others. This book would not be this book without her. Merci, Danielle.

I also thank Danielle for connecting me to Katherine Myers and Angelo Spoto. The daughter-in-law of Isabel Briggs Myers, Katherine sought, through a series of annual retreats with Angelo Spoto, to "reconnect the branch (MBTI®) to the tree (Jungian psychology)." Author of *Jung's Typology in Perspective,* Angelo significantly deepened my understanding of Jung's work. From the day he shared his theory of type development, revealed in this book, I realized how it applied to my life, and how it could help leaders. He read my nearly finished manuscript, and gave me treasured feedback. I hope this book motivates him to publish his model. Thank you, Angelo.

Many others in the type community have shaped my knowledge of type, for which I am very grateful: John Beebe, Linda Berens, Katherine Hirsh, Sandra Krebs Hirsh, Linda K. Kirby, Jane Kise, Laurie Lippin, Mark Majors, Raymond Moody, Elizabeth Murphy, Dario Nardi, Roger Pearman and Sharon Leibowitz Richmond. Vicky Jo Varner read the chapter on Thomas Jefferson, and gave me penetrating insights about introverted intuition (my shadow, her dominant). Thanks very much, my type guides.

Bob Saggers has known about my idea for this book longer than anyone. He has been a friend, colleague and encouraging accountability partner. I especially appreciated his detailed review from multiple perspectives: lifelong learner, MBTI practitioner, McGill University instructor, and leadership development consultant. I finally finished my book, Bob!

Colleagues and leaders throughout my life have shaped my understanding of type, leadership and/or myself: Brian Allen, Eva Andreassen, Rita Bailey, Rita Bayron, Dinah Chesson, Ron Elliot, Eleanor Goodwin, Brigitte Iafrate, Carrie McHale Reed, Mary Ober, David Ozment, Bill Prince, Helanie Scott, and Jane Winge. I especially appreciate my fellow LCC trainers from around the world: those coaching questions you posed me in Stockholm two years ago spurred me to finish this. Thank you all!

I thank Michelle Morse, my publisher, and her team. Without Michelle's deadline-driven demands, I might never have finished this book. Napoleon Hill said, "A goal is a dream with a deadline." I had a dream; Michelle gave me deadline after deadline, helping make my vision a reality. Marty Holtman reviewed a near-final draft from a fresh perspective, and contributed important changes, even then.

I want to express my deepest thanks to my family and friends who have challenged, prodded and encouraged me. To my mother, Marie, my brother, Drew, my sister, Margo, my son, Jared, my daughter, Jillian, and so many others in my extended family, thank you for your love and support. And to Patrick McBride, my spiritual leader-coach and greatest encourager, thank you for always being there, and to his son, Brandon, for the story about Truman. Finally, I want to thank Isaac Lobo for creating a space in which I could finish this book. I love you all. You helped make this happen!

Finally, while many people provided valuable insights, input and review, I acknowledge this work as my own.

Table of Contents

INTRODUCTION

WHAT DOES IT MEAN to lead? What makes someone a leader? How would you describe a leader you willingly would follow? (Give yourself a moment to reflect on that last question.) These and similar questions have been asked by leaders, followers, and philosophers throughout history. Countless biographies, memoirs, sacred texts, leadership tomes, and blog posts have produced literally countless answers. So, after centuries of exhaustive exploration, can we finally accept the answer: Leadership is incredibly subjective. It means different things to different people. It means different things in different countries, contexts, and cultures. It even looks different in the same person, depending on the situation, task, or role, among many variables. But, I believe, the strongest driver of how you will define and do leadership is your personality, and more specifically, your personality type.

Given the same situation, leaders of different personality types will see it differently. Even seeing it as a challenge or as an opportunity is an aspect of one's personality type. Even if agreed on perceiving the environment as a problem (or as an opportunity), different types of leaders will approach that problem (opportunity) differently.

Some will use an emergent, wait-and-see method (which may strike others as no method at all), while others will impose their solution on the circumstances. Leaders lead in countless ways. And, if they evolve and grow over their lifetime they access different skills to varying degrees and exhibit different aspects of their personality, almost seeming to become different people later in life. All, I believe, driven by their personality type.

That people with different personality types lead in different ways should be no surprise. You've undoubtedly watched as one leader in your organization relied on his intuition to guide his approach, while another focused on her consensus-building skills to get people on board, and yet another swung immediately into action with a can-do, just-make-it-happen tactic. But, if you're intent on building your leadership brand, you must have asked yourself some key questions: Which method works best? Which type of leader is the best? And the natural follow-up to that question: Am I that type? Of deeper concern might be, what type is favored in my organization? Do I need to be a different kind of leader to 'succeed'?

As someone who spends his life helping people build their leadership capacity, these questions are central to my work. Curious to find an answer, I embarked on a research project to explore leadership using the lens of personality type. I coupled this with my fascination for politics—not surprising for the son of a Louisiana politician to whom this book is dedicated. During the last twelve years I developed eight different profiles of leadership, each of which I call a LeaderType™:

Prudent: a stabilizing, conscientious guardian who leads with information and practicality

Proactive: an action-oriented realist who leads with a sense of urgency and pragmatism

Innovating: a pioneering, transformative catalyst who leads into the 'new' with inspiration

Visionary: an enigmatic, inventive prophet who leads with prescience and purpose

Inclusive: a caring, self-deprecating servant who leads with values and empathy

Persuasive: a tactful, collaborative influencer who leads with dialogue and encouragement

Take Charge: a delegating, results-oriented driver who leads with principles and conviction

Independent: a resolute, self-reliant thinker who leads with clarity and critique

Do you already recognize your LeaderType(s)? Which ones do you see elevated in your organization? In alphabetical order below are the eight presidents profiled in this book. Can you match the president with his dominant LeaderType?

John Adams   Franklin Roosevelt
Andrew Jackson   Theodore Roosevelt
Thomas Jefferson   Harry Truman
Abraham Lincoln   George Washington

The LeaderTypes for each president will be revealed in the next chapter. While my focus in this book is white, male political leaders in the U.S., I have seen all eight demonstrated in leaders—female and male—from Boston to Bangalore to Beijing to Bogotà, et al. My experience and the underlying theory would suggest this personality type-based system is universal. For skeptics, let me clarify what I'm <u>not</u> saying, and respond to potential questions or assumptions:

- I am <u>not</u> saying that you—or any leader—display only one of these LeaderTypes. In fact, **you have all eight of these in you** to varying degrees which recent research confirms. (See Appendix 6.) What I am saying is one will be stronger than the others, and serve as CEO, driving your leadership style. One or two others will support your dominant LeaderType. The unique combination of LeaderTypes you bring to a role, usually two or three working as a unit (e.g., Visionary-Persuasive), comprises your leadership brand. The remainder will be utilized to varying degrees, but one LeaderType will be very challenging for you, and likely be your Achilles heel in leading.

- I am <u>not</u> saying that context doesn't matter. It matters a great deal. In fact, I believe **one driver of your success will be how well your LeaderType fits your challenge**: that circumstances demand what you bring to the table; that how you naturally lead is what's called for, so that you are able to leverage your LeaderTypes to their fullest.

- I am <u>not</u> saying culture doesn't matter. I believe **leaders create a culture around them**, but I also believe that culture is shaped top-down. We look to leaders above us for clues on how to succeed. Many leaders below the C-level struggle to bring out their true LeaderType(s) because the organizational culture says to be 'successful' you must conform to a certain type. A senior female executive at a client shared this telling observation: "Cash, I always come out INTJ on the MBTI, but I also know the management culture here is INTJ, and I wonder if that's really my type." Consider whether your organizational 'mask' may be hiding your authentic leader-self, and thus limiting your effectiveness and your growth as a leader.

- I am <u>not</u> saying your personality type is static—quite the contrary. LeaderType is not about putting you in a 'box.' Organizations, however, can and often do. Their need for functional specialization may be at odds with your need for development. Your job may only demand one or two of your eight LeaderTypes. The longer you stay in that role the more proficient you become, but the more atrophied your non-used LeaderTypes will be. Taking on different roles and responsibilities requires you to **develop leadership capabilities outside your comfort zone** where much learning can happen. LeaderType acknowledges that you need challenges and change in order to grow and develop.

- I am <u>not</u> saying you can't—or shouldn't—develop skills outside your dominant LeaderType strengths. "You can't expect me to do team building, I'm an Independent LeaderType," one leader said, trying to get out of a session. What I am saying is that **some**

skills and behaviors will be more accessible to you at certain times in your life than others — and knowing that can help you be more deliberate about when you work on which leadership capabilities. Building and leveraging the natural leader in you will make you a more authentic, intentional leader.

Paraphrasing Jung, **every leader is an exception to the rule** — but you must first know the rule to which you're an exception. That rule is your dominant LeaderType. It rules your leadership. And it has a set of rules by which it operates. And although you will share much in common with leaders having the same dominant LeaderType, your version will be unique. To paraphrase Mary McCaulley, a pioneer in the type community, every Innovating leader is like every other Innovating leader is like no other Innovating leader. A base of commonality, however, will prevail. Your dominant LeaderType, as ruler, forms the foundation and core of your leadership brand.

Many factors that transcend LeaderType (e.g., intelligence, competence, business acumen, organizational savvy, et al.) can impact a leader's performance. While important, those are not going to drive that leader's day-to-day style: how she approaches leading others. A leader's LeaderType(s) will drive her way of leading: where she focuses her attention, what information she trusts, what she emphasizes (and doesn't), how she approaches and engages others, and how she makes decisions. Those are important things to know about a leader. Let's see how eight very different LeaderTypes have shown up in the U.S. presidency.

WHY STUDY PRESIDENTS?
WHY THESE PRESIDENTS?

It only makes sense to look to presidents — who we elected to lead us — for clear examples of different leadership styles. Even though the ones studied are of the same race and gender, I found incredible diversity in their personalities, not to mention all 42 U.S. presidents in the database. (See Appendix 1 for more about the database and my methodology.) And what better way to dissect 'good' leadership than in the lives of those whom historians have deemed some of our greatest? Here's why I chose to profile U.S. presidents in general, and the eight chief executives in this book, in particular.

- **Each is very well known.** Hundreds of books — thousands in the case of Lincoln — have been written about them, enabling a more objective, comparative analysis in their historical context. It also helps limit any individual historian or biographer bias. Plus, sixty-five years have passed since the last held office. The impact of these leaders has been established. Their history has been written.

- **Theirs was not leadership by fiat or force.** Citizens willingly followed them. Even Lincoln, who won the presidency with only 40 percent of the popular vote — but an overwhelming Electoral College victory — was the choice of a plurality of the people. These are not bureaucrats, technocrats, or managers who climbed to the top of an organizational pyramid within a distinct corporate culture and/or were named by a board of directors. These eight men rose to the office through their personal leadership, political savvy, and sheer will.

- **They served without a large White House staff.** With the rise in a large policy-making, image-shaping apparatus around U.S. presidents in the last sixty years, it can be harder to distinguish a president's personality type from the 'spin' put on them by staffers. (President Donald Trump, a notable exception to this rule, prefers to communicate directly with people via Twitter. As a result, his personality is visibly on display. He, in effect, spins for himself.)

- **These eight presidents were clearly driven by their personality-type preferences.** I will show how their styles—and sometimes even the policies of their administrations—were a direct expression of their dominant LeaderType. I will also highlight examples of their type development—some to a greater degree than others—showing how all eight LeaderTypes were present in all eight presidents.

- Through numerous rankings, **historians acknowledge these eight as 'great' or 'near great' leaders.** In other words, their lives and their presidencies were consequential; they shaped this country—and in many cases, the world. Their leadership made a difference. Therefore, they are worthy of study for what made them 'successful,' to derive useful leadership lessons. To choose these eight, I went back to the Murray-Blessing survey of 1982—a time when presidential rankings were less politicized. Another reason is that the Murray-Blessing identified historian-rankers as 'conservative' or 'liberal.' Interestingly, at that time, **liberals and conservatives agreed on nine out of the top ten.** (Woodrow Wilson is the only one not profiled here.) In that survey, liberals put LBJ in the top ten; conservatives, Eisenhower. The eight profiled here are from the agreed-on top nine. (See the Appendix 2 for the two rankings.)

My conclusion: After analyzing the psychological assessment results of forty-two presidents completed by 120 historian-experts, translating this data into personality type preferences, reading numerous biographies, and studying these men in their own words (autobiographies, books, diaries, essays, letters, speeches, quotes), **each of these eight 'great' or 'near great' leaders had a different, dominant LeaderType.** My message to leaders: No matter what your personality type, you can be a great leader. Just don't try to be someone you're not. Fully embrace your true LeaderType. Acknowledge that fundamental aspect of your leadership style — with all its pluses and minuses — and craft your own personal brand. **Be the unique exception to your rule.**

SELF-AWARENESS IS THE FIRST STEP

I believe exploring leadership through the lens of the presidency can be particularly helpful for a developing leader. If leadership is about accomplishing things with and through others, each of these eight demonstrated that in a unique way. There are specific lessons to be learned from all eight of these leaders — as well as in the patterns that transcend them all. And, I'm confident you'll find important takeaways in the profiles of leaders with whom you most identify. Looking in a mirror, metaphorically, is one way to build your self-awareness. Realizing strengths in common, acknowledging blind spots you share, and comparing the arc of their development with your own will hopefully help you learn more about yourself. **Before you can lead others, you first must lead yourself. And before you can lead yourself, you must understand yourself.** Understanding yourself helps keep you from derailing as a leader. A quote often attributed to Warren Bennis, leadership expert and author of *On Becoming a Leader,* confirms why you should know yourself: "The lack of self-awareness is the single greatest source of leadership failure."

An important 2010 study by Green Peak Partners and Cornell's School of Industrial and Labor Relations backs up the emphasis on self-awareness suggested by Bennis. After studying seventy-two executives at public and private companies with revenues from $50 million to $5 billion, researchers determined that, "Leadership searches give short shrift to 'self-awareness,' which should actually be a top criterion. Interestingly, a high self-awareness score was the strongest predictor of overall success."

Harry Truman said, "In reading the lives of great men, I found that the first victory they won was over themselves...self-discipline with all of them came first." Again, before you can manage others, you must manage yourself. My hope is that by reading this book and identifying with one or more of these eight presidents you can better leverage a strength, mitigate a weakness, reduce a blind spot, clarify your brand, live your values, be more authentic, and have more confidence in your capacity to lead. Best of success to you!

CHAPTER ONE:
Leadership is...

BECOMING A LEADER

IF YOU'RE READING THIS BOOK, chances are you are a leader—or aspire to be one. I believe wanting to be a leader is a first step toward becoming one. One common denominator I found among all eight Presidents was ambition. Leadership begins with a desire: the will to shape one's world, overcome a challenge, influence an outcome, or achieve a result—even if leading oneself. Whether it's disciplining and preparing yourself to climb Mt. Everest as a Russian student-colleague of mine did, or leading community conversations aimed at changing racial perceptions as a female friend is currently doing, leading others begins with leading oneself by taking action toward an ultimate purpose.

> *Becoming a leader is synonymous with becoming yourself. It's precisely that simple, and it's also that difficult.* WARREN BENNIS

Besides wanting to be a leader, wanting to be a *better* leader is, I believe, the most important driver of your eventual success. (Read the chapter on Abraham Lincoln for the epitome of self-improvement.) Twenty years of developing leaders have taught me that while some people may seem to have a natural predisposition for leadership, everyone can get better at it—and, let's face it, **our world needs better leaders** at all levels of society. With all due respect to President Harry Truman who said, in his book about great leaders, "You can't breed or teach leadership; it comes about naturally," I would add: "**Each leader's 'natural' is different, and every leader can and should learn to get better.**"

While developing yourself as a leader begins with realizing what you naturally bring to the job, it can't end there. Next comes self-management: Beyond accurately assessing your assets and liabilities, you must intentionally choose which natural talents to leverage and enhance—and which just-as-natural limitations to develop, delegate, or mitigate. I hope you'll nurture your natural predisposition to lead, and build your brand with the help of this book.

Sadly, too many people are failing to effectively use information about themselves to help them lead, often making them ill-equipped to manage others. In fact, according to research conducted by global management consulting firm CEB Gartner, a full 60 percent of new managers fail within the first twenty-four months of their new position, often, I believe, because the best doer is placed over other doers—irrespective of basic leadership skills or even leadership potential. Time after time, this leads to micro-management. The thinking of the newly appointed manager goes something like this: "Why else would management have promoted me, unless it was to make sure everyone does it my way..." What's worse, most new leaders are sadly unaware of what will make them successful—and what could potentially derail them. The title of Marshall Goldsmith's book speaks profoundly to new leaders: *What Got You Here Won't Get You There.*

About learning, let me quote a president not featured in this book, John F. Kennedy: "**Leadership and learning are indispensable to each other.**" (Historical and personal footnote: Kennedy never spoke these words. They were in his prepared remarks to be given in Dallas on November 22, 1963. As a sixth-grader I chose, of all the presidents, to research, write, and deliver my first speech on JFK.) This quote speaks to me in two ways: leaders have a responsibility to be continual learners; and once you learn something as a leader, you have a responsibility to lead that way. If you know better, lead better. Those who follow you deserve the best leader you can be.

I would add that even the timing of your leadership development matters. Carl Jung said, "Life really does begin at forty. Up until then you are just doing research." I believe there is a dynamic, cumulative learning process to life, and that people come into an awareness of and accessibility to all eight of these LeaderTypes over an average lifespan—if they choose to. Given someone's 'best-fit' type (the one out of 16 which, overall, comes closest to describing your personality type), I believe that process is predictable. If correct in determining your type, and assuming the theory holds true, certain talents will be more easily developed at certain stages of your life. (See the Appendix 7 for your predicted LeaderType development path based on your MBTI® type code.)

Each chapter will focus more on the early life of that president than on their presidency. James MacGregor Burns, leadership thought leader, says the most important influences on the shaping of leaders lie "almost wholly in their early years." Jung said, "If a plant is to unfold its specific nature to the full, it must first be able to grow in the soil in which it's planted." What soil produced these presidents? Burns' study of outstanding leaders revealed they were "subject to feelings of insecurity and lack of self-esteem," and that most developed an overarching ambition lasting their entire lives (which my research confirms). Many have a strong attachment to their mother. Freud reiterates this in *The Interpretation of Dreams*: people who are "preferred or favored by their mother give evidence in their lives of a peculiar self-reliance and an unshakable optimism which often seem like heroic attributes and bring actual success to their possessors." This was true for at least three of the presidents profiled here: Lincoln, FDR, Washington (double in Lincoln's case, as it was his mother and stepmother.). Most scholars would agree these three were America's greatest. So, be mindful, mothers: a president could be in the making. (And to my mother I say, "Thank You.")

THE FUNDAMENTALS OF LEADERSHIP

Here are some fundamentals I believe every leader should know. These are things I've learned from following my father and other leaders, leading myself and others, studying leadership, and teaching thousands of leaders around the world.

Leadership is Diverse and Subjective. Remember the questions at the beginning of this book? If I were to ask you to describe "a leader you would willingly follow," and compared your list of traits with the lists of a roomful of people, I'd bet *not one trait* would be common to half the lists in the room. We know a leader when we see one, but finding a generally accepted definition or description of an ideal leader is much tougher. Why? Because we perceive leaders through the lens of our own experiences, expectations, needs, preferences, and biases. **Leadership is largely in the eyes of the follower.** And yet, most leadership autobiographies or tomes are written from one leader's perspective, essentially saying, "Do it my way because that's what worked for me." Those books often reveal more about the author's personality type—and his/her persona, biases, and projections—than they shed light on essential truths about leadership. **One-size-fits-all leadership fits no one—except that leader.**

What does this diversity of leadership styles and subjective expectations of leaders mean for you? It means when your boss tells you to "Take the lead on this," make sure you know what she means. How is <u>she</u> defining leadership? How do you define it? It also means you must be clear with followers about how you lead: what you stand for, what your strengths and weaknesses are, and what they can hold you accountable for and expect from you. Understanding your LeaderType profile enables you to clearly articulate this: to define your leadership style, and set followers' expectations rather than letting them be set—not to mention set differently by each follower!

Leadership is dynamic and situational. Leadership happens within a specific context, time, and space—even if only virtual. A successful leader in one domain will not necessarily be successful in another. Consider Winston Churchill during World War II versus postwar. Historians generally agree he was a much more effective leader during the conflict than he was after that challenge had passed. The eight leaders profiled here faced drastically different worlds from each other, even when leading in adjacent terms. Today, multiple, divergent stakeholders, disruptive competitors, and constantly changing environments—most outside the leader's control—create what the Army War College has called a VUCA world (volatile, uncertain, complex, ambiguous). To remain effective, leaders must be able to successfully navigate complexity across multiple contexts. And those players and variables are constantly changing, demanding leadership agility. Knowing which LeaderType to bring out in which situation—*and how*—helps you be a more intentionally agile leader.

Leadership is complex and ambiguous. Not only is a leader's world increasingly VUCA, leadership itself is, largely because "people persist in being human," to quote Peter Drucker in *Managing Oneself* (a *Harvard Business Review* must-read for purposeful leaders). Because leadership is essentially about working with and through people, it's a messy complexity. With all that messiness, most leaders fall into the trap of taking shortcuts or filling in missing information. They make assumptions, infer motives, and/or project their needs and agendas onto others. Because much of this is largely unconscious, they're acting and reacting out of their "unknown unknowns" when it comes to dealing with people—not a good idea when you need to get the best out of them. The LeaderType system encourages more conscious, intentional "System 2" thinking (From Daniel Kahneman's *Thinking, Fast and Slow*, "System 2 [slow] allocates attention to the effortful mental activities that demand it..."). The LeaderType system provides a template to categorize and understand leadership in various contexts, thus breaking down the complexity. It can help you operate in more deliberate, cognitive ways, rather than reactive, unconscious ways. Knowing from which perspective or LeaderType you are operating helps you lead more thoughtfully. It also gives you clarity amidst overwhelming ambiguity. **And if navigating ambiguity and complexity are requisites for leaders today, think how much more critical they will be in an increasingly VUCA future.**

Leadership is about ends and means. Whether you call the "end" a goal, wanted position or vision, it's where you want to be at the end of the day. The ways in which you move people from where they are (point A) to that end (point B) are your means. "Means" typically means some generic form of influence—push/pull, formal/informal, intrinsic/extrinsic—or a more personalized method (leading by example, using data/logic, communicating benefits/values). Whatever the means, it must be sufficient to overcome the inertia of the status quo, and get people moving. Knowing your dominant and supporting LeaderTypes can help you realize your natural emphasis (on ends or means), and help you better balance the two, leveraging the LeaderType called for depending on where you are in the process of leading. **Your dominant LeaderType will also help explain which means you are likely to employ and which ends you are apt to target.** It will also give you an idea of what you communicate, as different LeaderTypes "trade" in different "currencies" (what they value and seek in the give-and-take of communication).

> *The task of the leader is to get his people from*
> *where they are to where they have not been.*
> HENRY KISSINGER

ELEMENTS OF LEADERSHIP:
THE PROCESS OF LEADING

After reviewing thousands of quotes on leadership, hundreds of models and theories, and more than a few definitions, I believe leadership can be viewed as **the process of moving people in a purposeful direction.** Whether at the self, team, organizational or national level, leadership implies energized movement along a path: How do I get my team and myself from point A to point B? Whether it's engaging thousands of employees in a multiyear, enterprise-wide culture change, reaching alignment within your management team around strategy, or getting one follower from "no" to "yes" in a difficult conversation, leaders move people. And in the process of moving others (or self) a leader must do four things. Every day, in multiple interactions each day, a leader must:

- **Grasp Reality.** Understand who you are and where you and your followers are. Confront the facts of your situation without bias. Acknowledge your mission/ task and available resources. Choose which strengths to leverage and weaknesses to mitigate in response to your situation.

As a leader you should always start with where people are before you try to take them to where you want them to go. JIM ROHN

- **Envision Success.** See, imagine, or visualize your group's desired outcome. Communicate it in such a clear and compelling way that people get it. Facilitate brainstorming to anticipate challenges. Point or pull them in a purposeful direction. Articulate the best way forward.

The essence of leadership is a vision you articulate clearly and forcefully on every occasion.
THEODORE HESBURGH

- **Engage Commitment.** Build mutual respect, rapport, and trust through real dialogue. Understand your followers. Help them realize what the journey will require, and how they stand to benefit. Secure their full and willing commitment, then nurture and sustain it.

Leadership is something you do with people, not something you do to people. KEN BLANCHARD

- **Drive Performance.** Clarify goals and expectations. Plan, assign, and prioritize tasks to achieve the target. Inspect what you expect. Communicate consequences of success and failure. Hold yourself and others accountable. Celebrate and reward accomplishment.

> *Leaders check performance... Leadership is defined by results, not attributes.* PETER DRUCKER

Think of these as the common denominators for all leaders. Your success as a leader, I believe, will be a function of how well you deploy these fundamentals. If one or more is neglected, leadership suffers:

- If your **Vision** isn't grounded in **Reality**, it will likely be perceived as fantasy. People won't follow a wishful, unrealistic dream — no matter how much they like or respect you.

- If you demand **Performance** without engaging **Commitment**, you may get people's compliance, but not their willing, discretionary effort. One truism I have witnessed among followers is this: Compliance does not equal Commitment.

- If you only focus on the **Reality** at hand and demand **Performance**, you will likely come across as a cold taskmaster, and fail to inspire or motivate your team.

- If you envision **Success** and engage **Commitment** without grasping **Reality** and driving **Performance**, you will likely be viewed as idealistic, and probably not accomplish much.

These four Elements are essential to leadership. Based on my experience, most leaders demonstrate one or two well, a third so-so, and the fourth is typically their Achilles heel — all stemming from their personality type. My intent is to help you: realize all eight LeaderTypes within you; own your unique leadership brand; and, apply all four elements to your leadership challenges — in each meeting or interaction every day. (For an app to help you balance use of all four elements, search LeaderCOACH® on the Google PlayStore and Apple iTunes store.)

CHAPTER TWO:
Personality Types
and LeaderTypes

Theories in psychology are the very devil. CARL JUNG

PAYING ATTENTION TO PATTERNS

RECOGNIZING PATTERNS IN YOURSELF and others—
and managing them—is what this book is about. It's
based on a theory developed by Swiss psychiatrist Carl
Jung, grounded in his observations of people—not just
patients, but acquaintances and colleagues, including
his one-time mentor Sigmund Freud. His purpose in
describing types: **"Giving some order to the apparently
limitless variations in human individuality."**

Jung and Freud split over their divergent views of human
nature. In trying to explain his differences with Freud and
Alfred Adler (another one-time member of Freud's inner
circle), Jung conducted an exhaustive study of literature,
history, religion, and philosophy, and came across the
type 'problem': that people can't help but see the world
according to their own type. His book, *Psychological*

Types, published in German in 1921, is considered one of the 100 most influential books ever written (according to historian Martin Seymour-Smith). His conclusion, that "every judgment by an individual is conditioned by his personality type and every point of view is necessarily relative," led him to a significant understanding not only about people in general, but about psychologists in particular.

Science requires the objective study of data from which hypotheses are made and conclusions drawn. In psychology, however, that which is being studied (the mind) is doing the studying. The observed is doing the observing. This makes objectivity difficult, if not impossible. This realization helped Jung dissect Freud's and Adler's theories: "Freud's view is essentially extraverted and Adler's introverted. The extraverted theory holds good for the extraverted type, the introverted theory for the introverted type." Anaïs Nin summarized the idea beautifully: "We don't see things as they are, we see them as we are."

Let the last paragraph sink in. Everything you perceive and conclude is filtered through the lens of your personality type. Now, realize the implication for you as a leader: Your perception of reality is just that, your perception. Your dominant LeaderType is the lens through which you see the world. And, others aren't necessarily (or even likely) to share the same lens. Now do you see the challenge of leading? How do you establish a common reality, not to mention a shared vision of the way forward? Yet, when dealing with the issues of our life, how many of us ever question our reality, much less seek out different—even opposing views? Usually, we fall back on "Well, that's just the way it is." Or we may comfort ourselves with the notion that our truth is <u>the</u> truth. Even if we consider alternative points of view, we usually end up concluding that our beliefs are correct because of cognitive dissonance. Attention bias, anchoring/insufficient adjustment bias and confirmation bias all serve to reinforce our pointed points of view. (For more information on biases, search Wikipedia for 'list of cognitive biases' where you'll find more than 150!) The very unsettling conclusion of much research on the brain is that, once formed, perceptions are extremely durable.

Furthermore, how you, as a leader, communicate and what you intend with that communication is not necessarily received as intended—especially across personality type differences among followers. Even though a Take Charge Leader may think she's doing 'what everyone expects,' followers may perceive it totally differently. **Your actions will be perceived through the personality type lens of your followers.** Even when conscious of our biases, it's another matter to think in completely opposite ways. Part of this book's purpose is to make you aware of fundamentally different ways people (and leaders) look at the world. **Once aware of these divergent worldviews, you'll be able to understand problems—and discuss them—from multiple perspectives.** The other benefit, to quote Isabel Briggs Myers, co-creator of the MBTI®, will be "clearer perceptions and sounder judgments"—something followers certainly want from their leaders.

WAYS OF SEEING THE WORLD

What are these different ways of seeing the world? Among Jung's many contributions to the world of psychology, his most famous was characterizing the opposite ways in which people direct their awareness and mental energy. Philosopher Joseph Campbell acknowledged his tremendous contribution: "If 'introversion' and 'extraversion' are standard words in most people's vocabulary . . . much of the credit belongs to Carl Gustav Jung." When directing one's attention and energy outward you are extraverting; when you direct that attention and energy inward you are introverting. Jung not only noticed patterns in how people are energized, but also in how they process their world. His model recognizes two cognitive functions every organism performs: *Perceiving*, taking in information, and *Judging*, reaching conclusions based on that information. Before going further, let me make something perfectly clear: **You do both every day. You extravert** (verb), **and you introvert** (verb). **You perceive, and you judge,** all day long. There are no pure types. It's only the relative predominance between the two which determines a type. Saying, "I'm an extravert (or introvert)" is misleading. Try this language instead: "My preference is for extraversion, but I can introvert too." **Introvert/Extravert is not who you are. It is what you do.** When people prefer one more than the other, and do one more than the other, we refer to them as having an 'extraverted' or 'introverted' preference. But that should never be seen as an absolute, only a tendency. Unfortunately, not clarifying that distinction has resulted in many people labeling themselves and others after a debrief of personality type results. Some in the type community—myself included—have regrettably contributed to this by reducing expression of one's preferences to an identity ("I'm an ESFP."), instead of saying "I have preferences for Extraversion, Sensation, Feeling and Perceiving."). I know this may sound esoteric, but it is essential to understanding what I am proposing in this book. Stating you are one or the other limits your self-awareness.

While personality manifests itself in a multitude of traits and behaviors, personality type is about preferences for mental processing. Leaders have personality types that reflect their preferences. Four of the presidents profiled were dominant Perceivers: their preference (i.e., bias) was to keep gathering information, and resist coming to closure. The other four were dominant Judgers: their tendency was to come quicker to a decision without perhaps gathering all necessary information. Four had preferences for Extraversion: their 'real world' was the outer one of people and events, giving scant attention to their inner world. Four had preferences for Introversion: 'reality' for them was their subjective inner world; the outer world held much less appeal. On a larger scale, organizations, institutions, and societies have collective personality types: they gather information and make decisions—over and over each day—until these patterns become "habits of the mind," an expression coined by Isabel Briggs Myers. These habits form a type.

Within these two basic cognitive functions, *Perceiving* and *Judging*, Jung saw another pair of opposites. When *Perceiving*, people tend to notice—and value—one kind of information over another. Either they focus on what they can literally sense (through sight, sound, touch, taste, smell, etc.), or they focus on what they intuitively perceive (through hunches, images, symbols, holistic patterns, etc.). Jung classified these ways of *Perceiving* as Sensation and Intuition. When using Sensation, someone is paying attention to input from her five senses; when using Intuition, she is heeding her sixth sense. **Everyone uses both their senses and their intuition every day**. If you primarily value input from your senses, and less so your intuition, you're a Sensation (or Sensing) type. If you trust your intuition more, but also heed your senses, you're an Intuition (or Intuiting) type.

Jung observed two basic ways people come to closure when *Judging*. He realized they made decisions based on either impartial principles and cause-and-effect logic (Thinking), or personal values and inherent worth (Feeling). Jung's labels for these processes sometime get in the way of understanding them:

- Having a Perceiving preference does <u>not</u> mean someone is perceptive.
- Having a Judging preference does <u>not</u> mean someone is judgmental.
- Having a Thinking preference does <u>not</u> mean someone has a strong intellect.
- Having a Feeling preference does <u>not</u> imply the person is emotional.

Jung called Thinking and Feeling rational functions because they involve judgment: coming to a conclusion about something—differing only in the criteria employed—your head or your heart. Again, **everyone uses both their head and their heart every day**. If you use primarily your head, and secondarily your heart, you're a Thinking type; if primarily your heart, and then your head, you're a Feeling type.

Jung used the metaphor of a compass to describe these opposite poles of mental processing, what he called functions of a personality (Sensation, Intuition, Thinking, Feeling), and that all four perspectives are required to get a holistic view of an issue or situation. Each of the points on the compass is energized by introversion and extraversion, so when multiplied times the four functions, they yield Jung's eight psychological types:

Extraverted Sensation	opposing	Introverted Intuition	} 4 *Perceiving* types
Introverted Sensation	opposing	Extraverted Intuition	
Extraverted Thinking	opposing	Introverted Feeling	
Introverted Thinking	opposing	Extraverted Feeling	} 4 *Judging* types

These eight form the basis for my LeaderTypes: eight ways of leading. An understanding of one's type preferences, and LeaderTypes, however, is only the beginning. Real leadership occurs when you can see situations from all eight worldviews, and from that deeper understanding, determine the best way forward.

WHAT'S A LEADERTYPE?

When you can access a function (Sensation, Intuition, Thinking, Feeling) at will, and use it over and over, you learn to depend on it. Jung noted, "(Our) habitual mode of reaction is normally characterized by the use of our most reliable and efficient function, which is **an expression of our particular strength**." Again, think of each function as being energized outwardly or inwardly (like a vector). The greater the energy, the more pronounced those LeaderTypes will be. Similarly, the clearer one's preference for a particular function, the more obvious the resulting LeaderType:

	Extraverted	Introverted	
Sensation	Proactive	Prudent	} 4 *Perceiving* LeaderTypes
Intuition	Innovating	Visionary	
Feeling	Persuasive	Inclusive	} 4 *Judging* LeaderTypes
Thinking	Take Charge	Independent	

Your dominant LeaderType will be the one that is the most conscious, accessible, and reliable for you. Clarity, however, about your LeaderType does not mean you're necessarily better at it. Even if your dominant LeaderType is Visionary (like Jefferson), it doesn't mean your vision is necessarily the right one.

Research by Dario Nardi, author of *The Neuroscience of Personality* and *8 Keys to Self-Leadership*, has correlated brain activity with these eight types: the four (4) dominant Judging types show more left-hemisphere prefrontal cortex activity (i.e., are more focused on decisions and explanations); the four (4) dominant Perceiving types show more right-hemisphere activity (i.e., are more attentive to process). Each of these eight types has a role in dissecting—and ultimately conquering—the issues and decisions of your life. Based on your cognitive preferences and personality type, one of these will be your most-favored approach. No matter what the subject or situation, using all eight can give you a 360-degree view, enabling you to make a more holistic assessment and reach a more balanced solution. Not taking into account one or more of these perspectives can result in a less-than-optimal decision.

One fundamental assumption in typology is a presumption of balance — between conscious and unconscious, extraversion and introversion, and perception and judgment. Here is the decoder from Myers-Briggs type to LeaderType, showing the dominant/strongest preference, as well as the supporting/auxiliary function of someone's personality type:

MBTI code	LeaderType		Dominant/primary function	Auxiliary/secondary function
IS_J	**Prudent**	}	introvert	extravert
IN_J	**Visionary**		perceptions	judgments
I_FP	**Inclusive**	}	introvert	extravert
I_TP	**Independent**		judgments	perceptions
ES_P	**Proactive**	}	extravert	introvert
EN_P	**Innovating**		perceptions	judgments
E_FJ	**Persuasive**	}	extravert	introvert
E_TJ	**Take Charge**		judgments	perceptions

This table helps explain how communication can break down between different types. An Innovating leader may extravert a possibility (perception), only to have opposite-type followers (Prudent) take that idea as a decision (judgment), or vice versa. It also explains why introverted leaders can be potentially disadvantaged when it comes time for performance evaluation: they extravert (or show) their auxiliary, or second-best, function. Their best function (i.e., greatest strength) is used in their preferred, inner world. Extraverts, on the other hand, are always putting their best foot forward: they show (or extravert) the dominant function of their personality type, their greatest strength.

YOUR LEADERTYPE AS A DRIVER

James David Barber wrote in *The Character of the President*, "Like any person facing extreme uncertainty, the President seeks within himself some ground of continuity, some identity he can recognize as his way of being." I think that way of being is another term for that president's dominant LeaderType. It's how he orients himself and processes his world. It is essentially his reality. And, that perceived reality — if he's the president — could shape the direction and destiny of a country. In organizations, it can shape corporate strategy and culture. That's why it's critical for leaders of a team, company, institution, or nation to understand their dominant LeaderTypes, as well as the LeaderType perspectives they may be missing.

Your dominant LeaderType functions like an operating system on a device, running multiple apps. For example, think of empathy as an app. How an Inclusive leader does empathy will be very different from how a Take Charge leader runs that app. Not only will it look and feel different depending on the LeaderType, even how the Take Charge leader 'installs' the app will be different. **Fully developing the leader in you requires you to know not only what works for you — and what doesn't — but how you learn best**. And that depends on your LeaderType. To get an indication of your top three LeaderTypes, go to www.leadertype.com.

WHAT'S IN IT FOR YOU?

By consciously recognizing and developing your leadership style, you create a signature brand with which to advance your career. That awareness boosts confidence, which fosters more opportunities to lead, and prompts others to value your contributions more. And if you continue to add value in your respective organization, it's likely you'll be recognized and rewarded for your leadership with greater opportunities for leadership.

Guidelines for Using Personality Type and LeaderType:

It's NOT a TEST! It's an INDICATOR! Its purpose is to <u>suggest</u> what you prefer, based on your responses. That's it. Typically, after receiving an explanation of the four dichotomies, and making a hypothesis about your preferences, you receive your **indicated** results. Whether the Myers-Briggs or Majors PTI™, you choose which type description (out of 16) best fits you. The Majors also gives you a result for all eight of the function-attitudes (which equate to LeaderTypes). Nobody (nor any instrument) can or should tell you what your personality type is, or what your preferences are. Full stop. Jung believed people were born innately predisposed to certain preferences, which may or may not be nurtured. Prior to responding to a type indicator, I suggest the following.

- Let go of any expectations (from work, home, or others) and 'shoulds' about yourself. This is especially important if you are responding in a corporate setting. When you know what the job description is, or what your boss likes, or what the culture expects you to be, then the potential for (unconsciously) responding that way increases.

- Mentally get to that place where you don't have to be anyone but you.
- Answer with what first comes to mind.

I believe approaching a personality type indicator this way will help you in your journey to discovering your true type.

- *LeaderType is not about putting you (or anyone else) in a box*. You have all eight of these LeaderTypes within you, in varying degrees of conscious awareness and use. You will share qualities with those with the same dominant LeaderType, but your unique combination of the eight is your brand of leadership. To quote Margaret Mead, "Always remember: you are absolutely unique . . . just like everyone else." Even Jung said simply categorizing people is pretty pointless. This is about increasing your self-awareness, not defining you.

- *LeaderType does not explain everything*. People defy categorization and prediction. No model or framework can explain every facet of human personality. George Box, a British mathematician, said, "All models are wrong. Some are useful." I have found Jung's theory of consciousness to be incredibly useful in understanding the limitless variation in people — and leaders. At the same time, type should not be used to explain things it can't. Realize that it is a tool that was intended for a specific purpose (primarily self-aware-ness), and should be wielded only by someone quali-fied in its proper use.

- *There are no better or worse LeaderTypes*. All are equally valid. Each offers a unique perspective on leadership; each comes with its own natural strengths and challenges; each has a role to play when leading; and each in its own time should be brought to bear when circumstances demand it. Don't let the corpo-rate culture tell you which type you should be.

- *Type-based preferences should never be an excuse*. People can and do use all their preferences every day at work. While the requirements of a job may run con-trary to your type's preferences — making some tasks more naturally challenging than others — all types can learn tasks in their non-preferred areas.

- *Personality type should NEVER be used to hire, fire, promote, or demote someone*. It is unethical to use the Myers-Briggs or the Majors PTI for such purposes. The decision of who to select for a position should be based on behavioral interviewing, and objec-tive review of prior results. Although there's a huge amount of research showing how satisfied certain types are in certain careers, it is not a predictor of job success. Past behavior and performance continues to be the most reliable predictor of future performance — not personality type.

Each LeaderType chapter follows a theory-example-ap-plication format. And even though it explains much about a leader's style, LeaderType is not all encompassing.

For that reason, other frameworks will be referenced in assessing each president's leadership.

David McClelland did landmark work in the motivational needs of leaders. He theorized three potential drivers of a leader's style.

- o **Need for Achievement**: desires significant accomplishment, mastery of skills or reaching high standards.
- o **Need for Affiliation:** desires the company and affection of others; values warm and close friendships; needs sense of belonging/identity with the group.
- o **Need for Power**: desires to have impact, influence on others — which can be used for the greater good of the organization or institution, or for selfish purposes.

In each presidential profile, I make a hypothesis regarding each president's motivational need(s).

Another important tool for self-understanding comes from David Rock of the NeuroLeadership Institute. His SCARF framework (Status, Certainty, Autonomy, Relatedness, Fairness) is helpful in categorizing the unconscious ways people are triggered. He posits that if one of these is a trigger for you, it works both ways: when positive it creates a 'toward' (or at-ease) state of mind; when negative, an 'away' state of mind (or threat response). Here's what each trigger involves.

- o **Status** – Where am I in the pecking order? Is my status relative to others elevated or diminished?

Daniel Goleman of emotional intelligence fame says the number one trigger to the brain is condescension or feeling disrespected (i.e., lowered status). Quite simply, the brain is wired for survival: the higher your status, the better your chances of surviving, for example, a corporate re-organization. Status can be based not only on power or privilege, but on competence, popularity, beauty, group identity or association, you name it. Our brains like it when we have status, and don't like it when we don't.

- **Certainty** – Do I know what's about to happen? What is this about? How long will this take? Our brains assume that what's happening now will continue to happen. This trigger is about needing to know what to expect. Plans are good. Surprises are bad.

- **Autonomy** – Do I have a choice in this situation? Do I have agency? The brain doesn't like to feel trapped. It equates choice with survival. Harking back to the Stone Age, you didn't want to get boxed in a canyon with no way out.

- **Relatedness** – Do I perceive those around me as members of my 'tribe' or not? This is a source of 'us vs. them' thinking. Being around 'your people' triggers affection and inclusion; being around those who are not your people triggers a threat response.

- **Fairness** – Did I just get the short end of the stick? Who came out ahead in that deal? Was that 'fair'? Your brain amazingly calculates this in milliseconds, and if Fairness is a trigger for you, your brain experiences a 'hit' — pleasure or pain depending on how you perceived it.

I find two or three of these trigger most people; your experience may vary. To take a free, fourteen-question indicator of your triggers, search "SCARF self assessment." Keep in mind these are ultra-quick, largely unconscious perceptions of your immediate surroundings. One area I wish to explore further on www.leadertype.com is the potential relationship between leaders' LeaderTypes and these triggers. I make a hypothesis in each chapter of that president's SCARF triggers.

- The type development model referenced toward the end of each chapter is based on the work of Angelo Spoto, a Jungian-trained psychotherapist and author of *Jung's Typology in Perspective*. He posits that someone's type develops in stages, with a particular, cumulative developmental sequence based on one's 'best fit' type (e.g., ESTJ). (See Appendix 7 for your order.) Your experience may vary, but remember, *you have all eight LeaderTypes in you.*

- The prominent qualities and deficits in the summary profile for each president are largely taken from the book, *Personality, Character & Leadership: Psychologists Assess the Presidents* (Rubenzer, Fascingbauer).

You've probably already noticed an extensive use of quotes. Points of view are a great way to Leadertype yourself. The more a quote resonates with you, the more likely it reflects that preference or LeaderType within you. And when one doesn't sound at all like you — or you react negatively to it — that may suggest your preference is its opposite. As Jung wryly suggested, **"Everything that irritates us about others can lead us to a better understanding of ourselves."** One caveat about the quotes: I am not implying the LeaderType or preference of the person being quoted. Their quote simply expresses that preference or LeaderType perspective.

Organized around the four Elements of Leadership are eight exemplar president leaders of each LeaderType. (See the Percentile Table in the Appendix 6 confirming their profiled LeaderType was the most prevalent of the eight LeaderTypes within them. In six out of eight cases, their dominant LeaderType represents the strongest display of that LeaderType among the eight.)

The 1st Element of Leadership: Grasp Reality

- Prudent   George Washington
- Proactive   Andrew Jackson

The 2nd Element of Leadership: Envision Success

- Innovating   Franklin Roosevelt
- Visionary   Thomas Jefferson

The 3rd Element of Leadership: Engage Commitment

- Inclusive   Abraham Lincoln
- Persuasive   Harry Truman

The 4th Element of Leadership: Drive Performance

- Take Charge Theodore Roosevelt
- Independent John Adams

Section I
The First Element of Leadership: Grasp Reality

The first responsibility of a leader is to define reality.
Max DePree

GRASPING REALITY IS HOW leaders confront the facts about themselves and their situation, and accept the challenge before them. It requires two often underrated leadership skills: observing and listening. Leaders must sense **what is** before they envision **what could be** or **what they want to be**. Like using Waze® or GoogleMaps® to map one's route, a starting location is essential. Often, however, this step is automated. Instead of assuming you automatically know your current location, you should intentionally give due consideration to where you are and how you got there, before setting a direction.

Leaders who excel at grasping reality in an extraverted way are attuned to their environment, and are quick to perceive threats and opportunities around them. The more-introverted graspers of reality easily identify their mission-critical strengths and weaknesses. Not surprisingly, Prudent and Proactive LeaderTypes' greatest contribution to strategy development is a SWOT (Strengths, Weaknesses, Opportunities, Threats) analysis. To be most effective at grasping reality, however, leaders must be conscious of their biases, and not let those impact their assessment of a situation or themselves.

What follows are two types of leaders whose forte was grasping reality — one in an introverted way (George Washington), the other extraverted (Andrew Jackson). Learn from these great leaders how to Grasp Reality — the first Element of Leadership.

Chapter Three:
The Prudent LeaderType
George Washington, 1st
President of the United States

THE PRUDENT BRAND:
DEPENDABLE GUARDIAN

YOU MAY BE WONDERING, why the word "prudent?" It may sound old-fashioned, but it describes almost perfectly the essential nature of this LeaderType. Another reason for the word (over several worthwhile contenders) is that Thomas Jefferson used it to sum up George Washington's character. Jefferson, an incredible student of human nature, knew Washington for almost four decades, going back to their service together in the Virginia House of Burgesses. Here is what he said of him: "Perhaps the strongest feature in his character was **prudence**, never acting until every circumstance, every consideration, was maturely weighed...His mind...was slow in operation...but sure in conclusion. Hearing all suggestions, he selected whatever was best... [but was]

slow in readjustment." That, in the words of a great leader himself, is the essence of the Prudent LeaderType.

Common sense is genius dressed in its working clothes. RALPH WALDO EMERSON

The word prudent conjures stability and dependability, but also caution and risk aversion. A Prudent leader builds a strong foundation from which to lead, offering security and reliability to followers. And that gift makes the Prudent LeaderType a guardian in any organization — but especially in one where this type is appreciated, even emulated, as the ideal. Followers naturally feel at ease, and can focus on the task at hand with a calm, stabilizing presence at the helm.

HOW THE PRUDENT LEADERTYPE FUNCTIONS

If steadfastness is this type's hallmark, the foundation is their deep knowledge of the subject, situation, or institution. Their chief currency is information. Their primary way of grasping reality is data, and lots of it, preferably sequentially stored for easy access. (If Excel® had been available in George Washington's day, he would have managed Mount Vernon — and the Revolutionary War — with spreadsheets.) Prudent LeaderTypes tend to trust their own sources. They rely on proven data established as fact. When in this mode, their minds focus inwardly, recalling past experiences in vivid detail. Consequently, they usually have impeccable memories. When confronted with new data, their approach is to compare and contrast it with their recall to establish the current reality. Finally, they monitor, audit, and verify any new information gathered as true or not. In one of many quotes highlighting this element of leadership, look how George Washington grasped reality: *We should . . . look back . . . to derive useful lessons from past errors, and for the purpose of profiting by dearly bought experience.*

PRUDENT LEADERTYPE STRENGTHS

- Tremendous repository of detailed, specialized, institutional or historical information

- 'Go to' resource for what's worked and not worked in the past, and how things should work

- Experience-based tactical approach; practical common sense; reliable, dutiful follower

- Attention to quality, accuracy, sequential order; steady, disciplined execution of a plan

- Following procedure; following up on tasks/training; following through on commitments

- Preparation, observation, documentation, organization, consistency, and due diligence

- Keen awareness of not only their own, but also their team's strengths and weaknesses

- Patience in explaining a task, providing guidance/ coaching, dealing with bureaucracy

History is a vast early warning system.
NORMAN COUSINS

PRUDENT LEADERTYPE STRUGGLES

- Dealing with unfamiliar situations; coping with missing data, inaccuracies, unproven 'facts'

- Acting or reacting with a sense of urgency; dealing with volatility, uncertainty, or ambiguity

- Dealing with others' inattention to detail, inadequate preparation, or random/messy work

- Integrating/adjusting to new/emerging information; status quo, anchoring, experience biases

- Not seeing 'the forest for the trees'; not sharing the context or 'big picture' with followers

- Specifying how tasks should be done; detailing procedures to follow; micromanaging

- Taking a too-cautious approach leading to risk-avoidance and/or neglected opportunities

Life must be understood backwards. But it must be lived forward. SOREN KIERKEGAARD

A PRUDENT LEADERTYPE IN THE WHITE HOUSE

For a look at how the Prudent LeaderType functions in real life, enjoy the following profile of President George Washington, the personification of the Prudent LeaderType.

GEORGE WASHINGTON, AMERICA'S FIRST LEADER

It is not hyperbole, I believe, to state that George Washington's Prudent leadership made this country possible. The fragile nation-in-making needed a rock-solid foundation on which to rely. The country needed someone with the strength of character and stability to lead the population through those first tumultuous years. As noted earlier, the Prudent LeaderType's hallmark is dependability, founded on an almost obsessive attention to detail. Followers know they can trust a Prudent Leader's grasp of reality, because it is invariably based on a mountain of data.

At a critical juncture in world history, when success depended on turning farmers into soldiers, newly minted Americans instinctively put their trust in the man from Mount Vernon. His physical presence demanded attention: a foot taller than most men (6'3") with straight-as-an-arrow posture and a piercing gaze, people literally looked up to him. François Jean de Chastellux, philosopher and soldier, said of him, "He excites… respect which seems to spring from the sole idea that the safety of each individual is attached to his person…The goodness and benevolence are evident in all that surrounds him, but the confidence he calls forth never occasions improper familiarity." That his troops believed he was their protector enabled him to hold together a band of poorly paid, ill-equipped, malnourished, disillusioned rebels that dark Valley Forge winter when all seemed lost.

Other factors were at work in forming his leadership brand beyond his Prudent LeaderType: Washington

craved power and expected deference to his authority. His need for power, however, was of the good sort,
according to McClelland's model. He was not self-ag-
grandizing, but directed toward the greater good of the
emerging nation. He sought "honor" (a term he used
often), which he saw as "disinterested, self-sacrificial service." And while he didn't enter the military for personal
gain, he certainly did so to build a reputation: He was
very ambitious, with a high need for Status: "The rank
of the office, to me, is much more important than the
pay," he was quoted as saying. He was a big believer in
strict discipline (Jefferson said, "His justice was the most
inflexible I have ever known."). And his bravery and
courage under fire are indisputable. ("...I had four bul-
lets through my coat, and two horses shot under me, yet
escaped unhurt, although death was leveling my com-
panions on every side of me," he once described battle
during his Proactive phase.) While courage and bravery
are not necessarily characteristic of all Prudent leaders,
these attributes certainly played a part in his winning the
hearts and minds of his loyal followers.

Arguably the most compelling aspect of his leadership —
despite his self-admitted human frailties — was that followers believed he had their best interest at heart, that
his intent was good. They, therefore, trusted his character
and selflessness (ethos); they shared in his commitment
to a noble cause (pathos); and they respected his abilities
(logos) — the trifecta every leader seeks. The proof of his
intentions can be found in what he ultimately did with
power: He was the first victorious general since the Roman
Empire's Cincinnatus to willingly relinquish power and

submit to the will of the people. (Interestingly, he was a student of Cincinnatus, frequently quoting him.)

He was determined, however, not to lose his moral compass despite his extraordinary influence and power. Keenly aware of that risk in accepting rule, as the first unanimously elected leader of the world's first democracy in 1,800 years, he said before taking office, "I hope I shall possess firmness and virtue enough to maintain what I consider the most enviable of all titles, the character of an honest man." Thomas Jefferson and Abigail Adams, separately, believed he succeeded; both called him a "great, good and wise man."

HIS PRUDENT LEADERTYPE ON DISPLAY

In true Prudent LeaderType fashion, Washington is widely known for keeping detailed notes on everything — the weather, eligible women at a party, crop records, his gambling debts, and most famously, his expense reports to Congress. Again, if he had had Excel, he would have documented the war with spreadsheets. Biographer G.W. Nordham described him as, "a conscientious and determined individual whose sound judgment won the highest respect because he sought out, listened to, and respected various viewpoints." As Jefferson said, "His mind was great and powerful, without being of the very first order; his penetration strong…and, as far as he saw, no judgment was ever sounder." On the negative side of the coin, all this data-gathering and perspective-taking resulted in him being notoriously slow to make up his mind.

The Prudent leader quality that most strongly character- ized Washington's personality was Conscientiousness (one measure of the noted Five Factor personality model). Expert biographer-historians rank him in the top 85th – 99th percentile of 42 U.S. presidents on all six Conscientiousness facets: competence, self-discipline, duty, order, deliberation, and achievement-striving. True to his Prudent LeaderType, Washington was cautious in planning and decision-making, and "inclined to gloomy apprehensions," according to Jefferson.

Washington's measured, deliberative style coupled with a keep-calm-and-carry-on demeanor engendered others' confidence in him. For example, despite his very limited military experience, he was named Commander of the Army. And, because the American Revolution was a defensive war (more England's to lose than the colonies' to win) where executing on tactics was more critical that an elaborate strategy, the job naturally played to George Washington's strengths. He advised, "On our side, the war should be defensive. We should, on all occasions, avoid a general action, and not put anything to the risk, unless compelled by a necessity into which we ought never to be drawn." His Prudent nature—and personal- ity type as a whole—was ideally suited to outlast a much better-equipped and trained force, and to compete in a drawn-out supply-logistics war, ultimately defeating the world's only superpower at the time.

The other most common observation about George Washington's personality was his reserved, formal, aloof manner—which I attribute to his preference for intro- version. It can be seen in other ways. He was highly selective in his friendships, often paraphrasing this line from Shakespeare's *Hamlet*: "Be courteous to all, but intimate with few, and let those few be well tried before you give them your confidence." Partly due to his introverted nature and the protection of his status, Washington didn't allow himself to get close to his subordinates—and discouraged them from doing so with their subordinates. My favorite quote from John Ferling's biography says it all: "No one ever kidded himself into thinking he was a friend of the commander."

MORE SIGNS OF PRUDENT LEADERSHIP

Further evidence of his Prudency can be seen in his presidency; he reserved activism for those situations where it was absolutely necessary to execute the Constitution. His preference for introversion also showed up in his means of influence: Washington preferred to work indirectly, through intermediaries, to accomplish his aims; he was the nation's first "hidden-hand" president, seeking to accomplish his goals behind the scenes. And if isolationism by a country can be viewed similar to introversion on a personal level, his introversion—and that of the next five presidents—all introverts—contributed to an isolationist philosophy in early U.S. history.

Finally, Washington was always conscious of the precedents he was setting, and prudently weighed how best to set them. This personality type frequently rewinds and replays history to grasp reality. Keenly aware that someone someday would do the same, he wanted the history he created to be viewed as, above all, sensible. In short, his dominant LeaderType matched the needs of an embryonic nation: as its Prudent father, Washington was perfectly suited to preserve, protect, and defend the new country until it could stand on its own.

HOW WASHINGTON'S LEADERTYPE WAS FORMED

Throughout his early life, young George was intent on identifying codes of conduct, memorizing rules, and emulating mentors, including his much older, half-brother Lawrence, and George William Fairfax, a neighboring planter. This required (and developed in him) some very basic, practical — yet often overlooked — leadership skills: observing, listening, studying examples, and reflecting on his own personal behavior. In other words, grasping the reality of one's own behavior compared to examples or benchmarks. I find this type puts extra emphasis on the need to lead by example. He also read, but almost entirely for utilitarian or self-improvement purposes. The book he most diligently studied (and copied, making it his own) was *Rules of Civility and Decent Behavior in Company and Conversation*, a compilation of 110 maxims for "proper conduct" assembled by 16th-century Jesuits for instructing French noblemen.

His early interests were typical for a boy of his day: hunting, fishing, living off the land, and horseback riding, all of which would serve him well in the infantry. His first job (at 16) was surveying and documenting wilderness territory, which helped him develop a great sense of direction and grasp of the terrain, resulting in a skill that would later help him plan his troops' marches to greatest advantage. When he initially joined the British forces (at just 22 and with no military experience to rely on), he was indecisive. While serving in the English army as an emissary, he honed his decision-making skills, learning to carefully weigh all information. He eventually learned to deal with his early indecisiveness, but more importantly, he came to understand the deficiencies of his soon-to-be enemies: English generals. These hallmarks of a Prudent LeaderType — his natural inclination to compare and contrast information, and thus grasp reality from multiple perspectives — resulted in his being vigilantly prepared to face the challenges presented to him.

Another way his Prudent LeaderType showed up early was in cataloguing his "foibles" — one of which was his temper. He focused his self-management on that specific aspect, and was able — for the most part — to keep his anger under control. Washington, thus, at a very young age, began crafting a brand. He aspired to be a "gentleman and a scholar" (more the former than the latter), studied how to become one, and developed himself into one by age 27: "I am now, I believe, fixed at this seat [Mount Vernon], with an agreeable partner [Martha Dandridge Custis] for life; and I hope to find more happiness in retirement, than I ever experienced amidst the wide and bustling world." While his retirement would be short-lived, this settling into a routine is reflected today in Prudent LeaderTypes' wanting to stay at companies or with institutions for a long time. They wish to build their knowledge; they tend to be focused on self-improvement; and they want to make steady progress towards their goals. When facilitating workshops at organizations with a strong Prudent-Take Charge culture I find that once given an assignment, heads go down. They diligently focus on the task at hand, and are meticulous about follow-through.

BEYOND HIS PRUDENT LEADERTYPE

Balancing Washington's dominant Prudent LeaderType (with its introverted Sensation) was Thinking. His second LeaderType, coming into conscious awareness and use, was Independent (See Chapter Ten for a full description.). That these two LeaderTypes were most active in his first forays into soldiering explains much of his indecisiveness: Prudent leaders can overwhelm themselves in a sea of data, attempting to 'boil the ocean,' while Independent LeaderTypes can argue—especially with themselves—ad infinitum a point for every counterpoint. Very common feedback for early-stage ISTJ leaders (like Washington) is the need to make faster decisions.

Washington's development of his Independent LeaderType coincided with his seeking to lead a life independent of his mother (an opinionated, possessive, controlling woman). He wanted to join the British navy, but his mother nixed the idea. She, however, approved of his becoming a surveyor. With a natural strength in mathematics, he ultimately secured an apprenticeship in surveying, and developed an expertise in a craft that would help him achieve independence from his mother. Another early sign of his Independent leadership was coordinating an expeditionary mission, where the shots he fired actually triggered the beginning of the French and Indian War. Outgunned and surrounded, he vacillated for hours over the terms of surrender, having to use a translator not as conversant in French as Washington thought him to be. Not surprisingly, he expressed regrets for trusting him. (Because Prudent types put great stock in the reliability of subordinates — especially their knowledge or expertise — this bothered him greatly.) It was also during this time that he clarified his thoughts about the English and the case for independence.

With his marriage to Martha he doubled the size of his holdings, and moved into a phase of life where his Take Charge leadership could develop. Management of Mount Vernon — experimenting with different crops, dealing with supply and demand, ultimately building it into a successful enterprise — was the perfect training ground for developing this auxiliary LeaderType. This George Washington quote summarizes perfectly the nuanced brand that combined Prudent, Independent and Take Charge LeaderTypes: "System to all things is the soul of business. To deliberate maturely and execute promptly is the way to conduct it to advantage."

To summarize the arc of Washington's development, and how each LeaderType showed up:

- **Prudent**: observing others' behavior, recording observations, itemizing, and documenting;

- **Independent**: developing expertise in surveying; clarifying in his mind the case for freedom;

- **Take Charge**: establishing structure and order at Mt. Vernon; executing expansion plans;

- **Proactive:** taking bold, courageous, agile action as the Revolutionary army commander;

His midlife struggle was whether to be who others needed him to be, and fulfill the much-needed, purposeful leadership of his country, or to retire to his life as a "gentleman and a scholar"; thankfully, he dutifully accepted the former responsibility in typically Prudent fashion, ultimately serving as our ex officio, colony-to-nation guardian leader for a total of 18 years.

- **Visionary:** his vision for Mt. Vernon, as well as his vision of a free nation, were fulfilled; (Note this quote during this time in his life: "I look forward with a kind of political faith, to scenes of national happiness, which have not heretofore been offered for the fruition of the most favored nations. The natural, political and moral circumstances of our nascent empire justify the anticipation.")

- **Inclusive**: initiating the presidential period when "he kept prima donnas together" (as one historian noted) for two terms; he realized the inclusive need for his Cabinet, as well as the nation; (While there has been much debate about Washington's religion, he made a particular point about religious tolerance, with a letter to the first Jewish community in Newport, Rhode Island, writing in 1790 after becoming President, "all possess alike liberty of conscience." He went on to say, "… for, happily, the Government of the United States gives to bigotry no sanction, to persecution no tolerance, requires only that they who live under its protection should demean themselves as good citizens…" Almost certainly knowing how Jews had been persecuted in Europe, Washington goes out of his way to deliver a definitively inclusive message to that group. "May the children of the stock of Abraham who dwell in this land continue to merit and enjoy the good will of the other inhabitants — while everyone shall sit in safety under his own vine and fig tree, and there shall be none to make him afraid.")

- **Persuasive**: encompassing his establishment of precedents and protocols, and of diplomatic relations; (He was a model of propriety, always choosing what was 'appropriate' with regards to custom.)

- **Innovating:** constituting his least-developed LeaderType, which can be seen in his wanting to be known for a 'bold, innovative stroke of genius' on the battlefield.

Thanks to his unique brand, George Washington looms largest of all leadership figures in American history. Just before his death, he himself noted how perfectly suited his Prudent personality was to that time in history. It speaks volumes to us today. "In times of turbulence, when the passions are afloat, calm reason is swallowed up, in the extremes to which measures are attempted to be carried; but, when those subside, and its empire is resumed, the man who acts from principle, who pursues the path of truth, moderation and justice, will regain his influence." George Washington, speaking from centuries before, makes the case for Prudent leaders today.

George Washington – Summary Profile

Leadership positions: Virginia militia; member, Virginia House of Burgesses; justice, Fairfax County; delegate, First & Second Continental Congresses; president, Constitutional Convention; commander in chief, Continental Army; president (1789 – 1797)

Age while president: 57 – 65

LeaderTypes:

Strongest: Prudent
Supporting: Take Charge, Independent
Emerging: Visionary (while president)
Weakest: Innovating

MBTI preferences (clarity):

- **Introversion** (moderate)
- **Sensation** (moderate)
- **Thinking** (slight)
- **Judging** (clear)

Prominent Qualities:	Courageous, Conscientious, Self-disciplined, Honorable, Ethical, Ambitious
Prominent Deficits:	Negative, Not Vulnerable, Overly Concerned with Reputation
Motivational need(s):	Power, Achievement
SCARF triggers:	Status, Certainty, Relatedness

COACHING THE PRUDENT LEADERTYPE IN YOU

If Prudent is <u>not</u> your dominant LeaderType, consider these questions to help nurture your latent Prudent LeaderType:

- What happened with respect to a particular situation or challenge?
- What can you learn from history or your experience? What worked? What didn't work?
- Given a current challenge, has anything similar happened before? How do they compare?
- How can you share institutional or subject-area knowledge easier or more conveniently?
- In what areas of work would better preparation, documentation, or standardization help?
- How can you stabilize the current situation? What routines could you put in place?

Prudent LeaderTypes tend to suffer from a deficit of extraverted intuition about their situation, as well as a tendency toward prolonged data collection and review to reach an optimal decision. Be aware of when you're operating in your best mode (Prudent), and when you're in the grip of your lesser-developed — even unconscious — LeaderTypes. If Prudent is your dominant LeaderType, consider the questions below to manage yourself better:

- How does your Prudent LeaderType show up? What does it look like in your world?
- How does this LeaderType get in your way? In what situations is it not called for?

- Who are your Prudent role models? How might they set a benchmark/standard for you?
- In what areas do you need to question your experience or data as no longer valid?
- What routines, procedures or processes are no longer needed? How to shut them down?
- Extrapolating the past into the future, what will likely become issues for you/your team?
- What future scenarios should you begin researching now to incorporate new data sooner?

QUOTES FOR A PRUDENT JOURNEY

I am a camera with its shutter open, quite passive, recording not thinking. CHRISTOPHER ISHERWOOD

God is in the details. LUDWIG MIES VAN DER ROHE

Beware the person who can't be bothered by details. WILLIAM FEATHER

It has long been an axiom of mine that the little things are infinitely the most important. SIR ARTHUR CONAN DOYLE

The only thing worse than learning from experience is not learning from experience. ARCHIBALD MCLEISH

Don't fix what ain't broken. BERT LANCE

Chapter Four:
The Proactive LeaderType Andrew Jackson, 7th President of the United States

THE PROACTIVE BRAND: ACTION-ORIENTED REALIST

PROACTIVE LEADERTYPES ARE ABOUT energy, activity, and speed. Their approach to situations is bold, enterprising, and agile. They quickly assess risks, and take necessary action, giving them a natural talent for handling crises and manifesting quick wins. Pragmatic facilitators when not dealing with an immediately critical situation they are the go-to people in organizations when things need to get done in a hurry. They bring a tremendous sense of urgency and realism to any role.

Among U.S. Presidents, Andrew Jackson exemplifies the Proactive LeaderType. He is often considered the first modern president, expanding the role from mere executive to an *active* representative of the people. He viewed himself as the direct agent of the common man, a concept that resonates to this day. In both administrative and military engagements, he was noted for strong, spontaneous action. This quote of his summarizes this type's approach: *Take time to deliberate; but when the time for action arrives, stop thinking and go in.* Knowing Jackson, the time he took to deliberate could be measured in seconds.

HOW THE PROACTIVE LEADERTYPE FUNCTIONS

The Proactive LeaderType focuses his energy and attention on what is: What's happening right NOW, and what happens next. Seeking information and stimulation from the environment, he focuses on external, sensory details to Grasp Reality. He instantly adapts to that reality and responds to the situation in the moment. His brain reveals a 'tennis-hop' pattern (according to Dario Nardi, cited earlier) that reflects how light-footed he is, ready to respond in a moment's notice. Employing a just-do-it mindset, he effortlessly reacts to the most pressing demand in his immediate surroundings. His ability to notice and internalize information sometimes makes his decision-making appear instantaneous. In a very insightful observation about this type Supreme Court Justice John Catron said of Andrew Jackson, "The way a thing should be done struck him plainly."

The Proactive leader is typically the consummate adventurer and thrill-seeker, often employing the motto, "Work hard. Play harder." He craves excitement—even danger—always intent on making things interesting. His need to avoid anything dull or boring drives him to (try to) multitask as a means of keeping things lively. Be certain that he will expect you to take on the mantle of multitasking and constant motion, so buckle up, and get ready for a thrilling ride.

We cannot put off living until we are ready. The most salient characteristic of life is its urgency, "here and now" without any possible postponement. Life is fired at us point-blank. JOSÉ ORTEGA Y GASSET

PROACTIVE LEADERTYPE STRENGTHS

- Experiencing reality 'in the moment'; instinctively reacting in competitive situations
- Grasping reality of external issues — especially immediate opportunities and threats
- Readily adapting to fast-paced, dynamic environment; managing crises; troubleshooting
- Conveying a strong sense of urgency and confidence when facing challenges or risks
- Implementing multiple projects or tasks — almost simultaneously — with speed, efficiency
- Facilitating effective group interaction; improvising the most expedient, feasible solution
- Persevering through barriers/obstacles until they get a solution, achieve the goal, or win

Face reality as it is, not as it was or as you wish it to be. JACK WELCH

PROACTIVE LEADERTYPE STRUGGLES

- Not seeing the long view, "big picture," or need for a strategic vision or long-range plan

- Not practicing impulse control; not reflecting on consequences before acting or reacting

- Having to follow detailed procedures; dealing with others' rigidity or micromanagement

- Becoming adversarial if their need for speed is not met—inactivity, solitude, boredom, impatience

- Prioritizing the urgent over the important; equating busyness with getting things done

- Seeking constant stimulation resulting in overstimulation or overindulgence if unchecked

- Not taking stock of self: deficient inner awareness, self-reflection, and/or personal vision

Tomorrow's life is too late. Live today.
MARCUS VALERIUS MARTIALIS

THE PROACTIVE LEADERTYPE
IN THE WHITE HOUSE

For a look at how a Proactive LeaderType grasps the reality presented to him, consider the following profile of President Andrew Jackson, a vivid example of the Proactive firebrand.

ANDREW JACKSON, BRINGING ACTION AND ENERGY TO THE WHITE HOUSE

A PROACTIVE LEADERTYPE TAKES CENTER STAGE BY STORM

Historian H. W. Brands said, "Andrew Jackson wasn't the greatest president, but he may have been the most important." The only president whose name was an era in history, Jackson's leadership was incredibly consequential: his example set the tone and template for many a president to follow. His Proactive nature—bold, experiential, and immediate—redefined the United States politically, economically, and socially. Andrew Jackson essentially led America's second revolution.

The first six presidents of the U.S. were introverted, mostly educated, aristocrats—all products of the Enlightenment, and all born in either Massachusetts or Virginia. For 50 years, the government had been steered by a select few, their succession predictable. Then came Andrew Jackson, and the contrast could not have been starker: this clearly extraverted, little-educated, poor son of 'Scotch-Irish' immigrants—whose passions often overcame him—was elected, representing 'everyman.' Decidedly not to the manor born, his financial success was largely self-made. (The one time he did inherit a considerable sum, at age 15, he spent it all in a whirlwind of wild living.) And while he studied and practiced law—and eventually became an enthusiastic reader—his educational interests (like Washington's) were strictly utilitarian. His political success derived largely from his war hero status (which he also had in common with only George Washington among the founders). But, what separated him more than anything from his predecessors was his pugnacious personality: an argumentative, populist, demagogue of Proactive-Take Charge leadership.

Populism is particularly prevalent among Proactive LeaderTypes in the political domain with good reason. They are constantly surveying the situation to see where threats and opportunities lie—in this case, among the body politic. Once having sensed the political landscape they are amazingly adept and agile in responding—some would say reacting—to their environment. In Jackson's case, riding the wave of popular will. Given Jackson's threat to the status quo it's not surprising that Thomas Jefferson, whose personality type was Jackson's exact opposite, called him "a dangerous man." Quoted early on, Andrew Jackson said of himself, "I know what I am fit for. I can command a body of men in a rough way, but I am not fit to be President." But once the force of nature that was Andrew Jackson stormed into Washington, neither the country nor the presidency would be the same.

Until 1828 power was in the hands of a few: Congress and the Supreme Court held sway; the United States was a democratic republic ruled by an influential elite of property-owners and financiers. Under Jackson, the essence of what this country was—and who could be president—changed forever. With his election the United States became a true democracy. ("If Andrew Jackson can be President, then *anyone* can be!" said someone familiar with him and his sordid past, revealing just how common a man he was.) But it was the bitter, divisive election four years earlier which set in motion his becoming the "People's President." The 1824 election was the first in which ordinary men could vote (in three-fourths of the states). Jackson won the popular vote; however, because no candidate won a plurality of electoral votes, the election was thrown to the House of Representatives. Henry Clay of Kentucky, who finished fourth, threw his support to John Quincy Adams. After winning the vote in the House, Adams named Clay Secretary of State (essentially heir to the presidency) in what became known as the "Corrupt Bargain." That only served to foment Jackson's followers' belief that power was too concentrated in too few and that unbridled self-interest among the rich and powerful had gotten out of hand. And Andrew Jackson, the epitome of a Proactive-Take Charge leader, was just the man to take the elite of Washington — and the bulls of Wall Street — by his powerful hands and correct that.

John Quincy Adams disdainfully described Jackson as "A barbarian who could not write a sentence of grammar and could hardly spell his own name." (Fact check: he was known to spell the same word differently — on the same page.) One of Jackson's longtime confidants remembered him as "the most roaring, rollicking, game-cocking, horse-racing, card-playing, mischievous fellow that ever lived." People either loved him or hated him. Someone even tried to kill him — the first presidential assassination attempt in U.S. history.

He had other notable firsts, as well as lots of quick starts (and some non-finishes) indicative of his Proactive nature: the first Senator from Tennessee (lasting six months in the job), the first Governor of Florida (lasting a few months), the first president to ride in a train, and founder of the modern-day Democratic Party.

Inevitably, Jackson defeated Adams in 1828 to become the seventh president. The victory was bittersweet for Jackson, as his wife Rachel, who had been deeply affected by the contentious campaign, died December 22, 1828, before he entered the White House.

A FIGHTER FROM AN EARLY AGE

He was a gangly—even fragile—youth, at six feet tall, and never weighed more than 145 pounds. Yet he was "always itching for a fight with anyone he felt was slighting or maligning him. Though he seldom won these adolescent battles, he constantly came back for more, taking on any boy, regardless of size or ability, with the kind of temper typically ascribed to a red-headed Irishman." (From *Presidential Courage.*)

Perhaps Jackson's anger was not entirely attributable to heritage. His childhood was an unimaginable horror of poverty, war, and death. His father died before he was born; his mother, Elizabeth, moved baby Andrew and his two brothers in with another family where she could work for food. Jackson's oldest brother, Hugh, joined the Revolutionary War effort, and died of heat exhaustion after a battle. When he was only 13, Andrew and his other brother, Robert, joined the army too. Both were captured and suffered sword wounds from a British officer whose boots Andrew refused to polish. Put into a prisoner of war camp with little food, no bandages or medicine, they both contracted small pox from which Robert later died. Elizabeth secured her boys' release, and Jackson walked forty-five miles home…in the rain…barefoot. His mother contracted cholera from attending to wounded soldiers, and died in 1781. Orphaned and a man at 14, Andrew Jackson emerged from his youth not only a skilled fighter, but also a survivor. He would harbor resentment of the British for life and eventually have the chance to avenge the deaths of his mother and two siblings.

His fighting in duels is legendary — perhaps somewhat exaggerated, but he carried a bullet to his grave from a duel defending his wife's honor. (The bullet was too close to his heart to remove.) This among many events suggests that in terms of emotional triggers the biggest for Jackson was Status. Any perceived slight incited him to challenge the person and re-assert his superiority. He was also triggered by Autonomy, often having difficulty with 'orders' or perceived controls on him. He was even fined $1,000 by a New Orleans court for his autocratic rule of the city. And he was triggered by Relatedness. He saw the world as us vs. them, friend or foe, and would always choose fight over flight. If you were deemed a friend, he would do anything within his power to help you (e.g., political patronage). But if you were a foe, watch out. He showed no mercy — no matter whether man, tribe, party, politician, institution, or nation.

HIS PROACTIVE-TAKE CHARGE LEADERSHIP ON DISPLAY

Like Washington, he made an early name for himself, and those who recognized his talents mentored him in his career. But, Jackson's reputation for brashness preceded him. He offered his services to President James Madison when the War of 1812 broke out, but was rejected due to his temper and association with Aaron Burr. He was eventually commissioned to lead 1,500 troops to Natchez, and then to proceed to New Orleans. When the immediate threat dissipated, and orders changed, he and his men were dismissed without compensation or the means to return to Tennessee. Vowing to pay his men's way home if the government wouldn't, Jackson endured a month-long march—allowing wounded soldiers to ride his horse while he marched—earning the respect of his men and the nickname "Old Hickory" (as in tough as old hickory wood) for sharing their hardships.

When the British threatened the Gulf Coast again, Major General Jackson was given command of the southern frontier. He prevented their landing at Mobile, and then marched toward New Orleans to defend it. On January 8, 1815, Jackson and his men won a lopsided victory (2,037 British casualties versus 71 Americans) at the Battle of New Orleans which was, as it turns out, avoidable: news had not reached America that a peace agreement had already been signed in Europe. But as a result, Jackson's status as a national hero was now second only to George Washington's. With the victory Andrew Jackson put an exclamation point on the Revolutionary War motto, "Don't tread on me": It was the last attempt by a foreign nation to invade the United States. Jackson said, "Peace, above all things, is to be desired, but blood must sometimes be spilled to obtain it on equable and lasting terms."

Jackson, was, in all things the epitome of energetic action, often overstepping boundaries—literally. He was called back into action to push the Seminole back into Florida (then owned by Spain), and went so far as to capture Pensacola, without authorization. Despite calls to reprimand Jackson, President James Monroe offered him the governorship of the new state, once it was purchased from Spain. His time as governor was short and combative. Upon his return to Tennessee, powerful friends nominated Jackson for the U.S. presidency in 1822 — although the election would not be for another two years — and elected him to the U.S. Senate again. In every area of his life, from his military career to his personal and professional life, and of course throughout his presidency, there is a staggering and nation-transforming amount of activity and change: economic, financial, sociological, technological, and of course, political. As a very clearly extraverted type, Jackson expanded the United States' borders and its trade with other countries.

THE JACKSON PRESIDENCY

Jackson's is often called the first modern presidency because of his belief that the president is not just an executive but a representative of the people, much like a Congressman but for all the people rather than those of a specific district, earning him the nickname "People's President." His Proactive LeaderType would suggest he sensed oneness with the body politic: he embodied their desires; they were a very real part of him. He was determined, on their behalf, to end government corruption, the Electoral College, and the nation's financial difficulties caused, he surmised, by upper-class elites.

In a classic 'us vs. them' fray early in his first term, Jackson's own cabinet members socially ostracized Secretary of War John Eaton and his wife over perceived social differences. Eaton had defended Rachel Jackson during the presidential campaign, and Jackson came to Eaton's defense. At the same time, many of his cabinet members thought he would be a one-term president and were trying to position themselves as candidates in the next election. To solve both problems, in 1831 Jackson dismissed his entire cabinet except for the postmaster general. The controversy caused him to rely heavily on a group of trusted advisors—called the "Kitchen Cabinet" because of the unofficial access they had.

When he determined that the "American System" of protective tariffs and internal improvement was no longer helping the country he essentially halted federal internal improvement spending, reversing himself on the tariff. In 1831 Jackson renounced protection and endorsed a reduction in rates. Invoking Jefferson, he urged a return to a simpler, more frugal, minimalist government.

Jackson also presided over the nation's first secession crisis. South Carolina declared the right to nullify federal tariff legislation because it hurt the state's financial interests and threatened to secede in November 1832, following Jackson's reelection. Jackson introduced a Force Bill to Congress that would allow him to send federal troops to South Carolina to enforce laws and prevent secession. The bill was delayed long enough for a compromise tariff bill to make its way through Congress. On March 1, 1833, both bills were passed and secession—and civil war— was narrowly avoided. President Abraham Lincoln would later cite Jackson's actions during the nullification crisis in his attempts to prevent secession and the Civil War.

Jackson's Proactive-Take Charge nature came to the fore in what he decided to do with the dwindling but significant number of Native Americans, and the ever-increasing number of African-born slaves. While these were not new issues, the direction Jackson's presidency took was particularly influential for the nation. Jackson believed that small family farms were the backbone of the American economy, and with population growth, new farmland was needed. His preference for action over philosophizing resulted in signing many treaties for removal of Native American tribes. Asserting they did not constitute separate nations, he drove legislation through Congress essentially saying if they wished to maintain their independent governance, they had to move west beyond established states.

The Indian Removal Act, passed in 1830, was ultimately used to force the removal of Native Americans from the South to the West throughout his presidency, opening land in the South to settlement and to a Georgia Gold Rush at the end of the 1820s. While Jackson's intent was not to destroy the Native American population, his insistence that the Cherokee nation and other tribes be removed beyond the then-frontier ultimately resulted in their decimation and near extinction. His actions (a fulfillment of Jefferson's original vision) reflected his grasp of the reality at the time: If left where they were with what they had (in weapons), the native population would fall victim to immediate genocide at the hands of white landholders on the cusp of manifest destiny. His Proactive type, challenged to think beyond the immediate crisis, could not foresee the denouement (his largely unconscious, least-developed Visionary LeaderType). The Trail of Tears (as the exodus from their native lands was called) would amount to the United States' first ethnic cleansing. Ironically, Jackson adopted a Native American baby boy whose mother was killed in a Creek War battle, and along with the adopted sons of his wife's brother, reared him as his own. His ability to empathize with another orphan of war makes sense, and yet it did not translate into empathy for the broader plight of Native Americans.

JACKSON'S IMPACT ON THE PRESIDENCY AND HIS PARTY

Jackson set many a mold that later presidents would emulate. Truman, in fact, called him the greatest president (coincidentally, they shared a strong Sensation preference), and modeled his 'kitchen cabinet' after Jackson's. Many have imitated his strongly populist philosophy — especially when stoking 'us vs. them' sentiments among the downtrodden against the rich and/or powerful. Countless candidates since have claimed rags-to-riches stories, promised reform, or vowed to put the will of the people—or rather, their interpretation of the will of the people—as an end justifying any means. Whatever their desired result, every president after Jackson, thanks to his example, exerted the full power of a democracy: expressing—and when authentic, personifying—the unambiguous will of the people. This resulted in a corollary feedback loop, in which, according to Barber, "[the] dramatic force (of his personality) extended electoral partisanship to its mass base." Jackson ignited a democratic revolution, and established the current-day Democratic Party.

BEYOND HIS DOMINANT PROACTIVE LEADERTYPE

Andrew Jackson's preferences were for Extraversion, Sensation, Thinking and Perceiving (ESTP). Here is the order in which his other LeaderTypes emerged, and how they impacted his leadership.

- **Proactive** – Jackson's early years were about survival, dependent on his awareness of his surroundings, and ability to act on the presenting situation to leverage his strengths.

- **Take Charge** – Fighting both personally and for his country, Jackson took charge of his life, setting in motion his career, studying law, becoming a lawyer and posting his twelve principles.

- **Independent** – Jackson defined and articulated his strong belief in individual liberty as a judge; this period was the genesis for many of his ideas, and his launch into politics.

- **Prudent** – Resigning from office, Jackson suffered several setbacks and focused on his personal life, marrying and adopting children, establishing his family and traditions. With the purchase of The Hermitage plantation, his ego was comfortably established. He was master of his domain.

His midlife crisis was the marked by the tension between his sedate, boring life, and the need to remake his himself and his reputation. Having been tarnished by association with the treasonous Aaron Burr, he brought himself out of 'early retirement' and into military service with the

War of 1812, forging a path to his life's second act: leading the country.

- **Innovating** – During this time Jackson met new challenges, and transformed his image via the winning of
  battles. This would be the catalyst for his being nominated to the presidency.

- **Persuasive** – When he needed to be, Jackson could
  be diplomatic and courteous. This Persuasive phase
  fortunately coincided with his campaign for election.
  His personal rags-to-riches story, his hero status, and
  people's ability to relate to 'one of them' helped elect
  him.

- **Inclusive** – Jackson's authenticity as a leader and
  trust in his inner circle paid off: he left office incredibly popular. One of his greatest accomplishments:
  paying off the national debt.

- **Visionary** – In his 1837 Farewell Address, Jackson
  prophetically warned of the dangers of sectional
  fanaticism, both northern and southern.

In brief, Andrew Jackson's legacy was a party rebuilt,
a Presidency redefined, and a nation reborn. Whatever
his faults, Andrew Jackson and his Proactive leadership
shaped these United States for centuries.

Andrew Jackson – Summary Profile

Leadership positions: Judge advocate general, Davidson
County (Tennessee) militia; major general, Tennessee
militia; major general, U.S. Army; attorney general,
Western District of North Carolina; delegate, Tennessee
State Constitutional Convention; U.S. congressman; U.S.

senator; Tennessee Supreme Court judge; governor, Florida Territory; president (1829 – 1837)

Age while president: 61 – 69

LeaderTypes:

Strongest: Proactive

Supporting: Take Charge, Independent

Emerging: Persuasive (while president)

Weakest: Visionary

MBTI preferences (clarity):

- **Extraversion** (very clear)

- **Sensation** (clear)

- **Thinking** (clear)

- **Perceiving** (clear)

Prominent Qualities:	Courageous, Assertive, Ambitious Jackson: "One man with courage makes a majority."
Prominent Deficits:	Anger/Hostility, Impulse control, Not compliant, Not modest, Not straightforward, Not trustworthy, Not altruistic
Motivational need(s):	Power, Achievement
SCARF triggers:	Status, Relatedness, Autonomy

COACHING THE PROACTIVE LEADERTYPE IN YOU

If Proactive is <u>not</u> your dominant LeaderType, you may wish to develop these fundamental aspects.

- What's going on around you? Be aware of your environment. Notice and identify specifics.

- What's up? What do you perceive? What's your immediate take on it? Instinctive reflex?

- Can you put yourself in situations where you must react immediately, with a sense of urgency?

- What's an action you could take—without thinking much about it—right now? Do it!

- What's the risk of not acting? What's holding you back? Think of the exhilaration in action.

- How could you reward yourself for taking this action? How to reinforce a quick response?

Jung said, "No other human type can equal the extraverted sensation (Proactive leader) type in realism. Since one is inclined to regard a highly developed reality-sense as a sign of rationality, such people will be esteemed as very rational. But in actual fact this is not the case, since they are just as much at the mercy of their sensations in the face of irrational, chance happenings as they are in the face of rational ones. This type…naturally does not think he is at the mercy of sensation. His whole aim is concrete enjoyment, and his morality is oriented accordingly."

If Proactive is your dominant LeaderType, consider these questions to challenge you further:

- How do you process your perceptions in the moment? How can you speed up your reflexes?

- How do you 'read' the landscape? How do you know which threat/prospect to tackle first?

- What's the next right thing to do? What can you do right now? What can you get away with?

- How do you assess risks? How can you incorporate future consequences into your decisions?

- What about tomorrow? Where's this headed? How will this play out a month or year from now?

- What does all this activity really mean? What's the personal significance or meaning to you?

- What's your personal vision? Life's purpose? Where do you want to be ten years from now?

QUOTES FOR A PROACTIVE JOURNEY

There is nothing worse than being a doer with nothing to do.
ELIZABETH LAYTON

For the things we have to learn before we can do them, we learn by doing them. ARISTOTLE

I learned that the richness of life is found in adventure... It develops self-reliance and independence. Life then teems with excitement. There is stagnation only in security.
WILLIAM ORVILLE DOUGLAS

The spur of the moment is the essence of adventure.
ANTONY ARMSTRONG-JONES

The only thing you live to regret are the risks you didn't take.
ANONYMOUS

Never tell me the odds. HANS SOLO FROM STAR WARS: A NEW HOPE

Carpe diem!

Section II
The Second Element of Leadership: Envision Success

I have a dream. MARTIN LUTHER KING, JR.

ENVISIONING SUCCESS IS ABOUT imagining the future, articulating a compelling vision, seeing the way forward, and being able to craft and communicate one's strategy. This second Element of Leadership requires foresight, creativity, and, in short, intuition. This aspect of leading gives direction and meaning to the journey.

Leaders adept at envisioning success can transport themselves and their teams forward in time, and give them a clear idea of what it will look like when they reach their desired outcome. Defining success in vivid detail — including how it will feel to succeed — is an essential skill for leaders. It enables you to pull people in your direction. It builds momentum for the journey. The strength of your leadership vector (energy x direction) is revealed in how well you Envision Success.

Let's look at two of America's greatest leaders, one extraverted (Franklin Roosevelt), and the other introverted

(Thomas Jefferson), and their capacity to inspire with their future-tense leadership. They epitomize the forward-looking requirement of leaders. They can show you how to Envision Success, and help you leverage the second Element of Leadership in fulfilling your mission.

Chapter Five:
The Innovating LeaderType Franklin D. Roosevelt, 32nd President of the United States

THE INNOVATING BRAND: NONSTOP CHANGE-MAKER

THERE IS NOTHING AS boundary-less as an Innovating LeaderType in action. Pioneers by nature, these leaders perceive no limits, and eat change for breakfast. They tend to be optimistic, expressive, and entertaining. They are masters at ideation: generating ideas, building on others' ideas, and re-fashioning ideas to produce fresh solutions to long-standing dilemmas. They are the future-focused "imagineers" of the world, constantly inventing, improving and transforming. They are the catalysts for redesigning whatever 'playground' in which they find themselves.

Among great U.S. presidents, Franklin Delano Roosevelt displays the Innovating LeaderType at a level rivaled only by his cousin, Theodore (profiled in Chapter 9). Faced with the devastating reality of the Great Depression, he convened a 'brain trust' to brainstorm ways to solve the greatest economic crisis to confront the United States. The solution—a New Deal reminiscent of his cousin's Square Deal, yet decidedly different — consisted of existing ideas and new programs to stimulate the critically ill economy. FDR reshaped the economic landscape of this country (his 'playground') such that portions of that solution—notably Social Security and Unemployment Insurance—survive to this day.

HOW THE INNOVATING LEADERTYPE FUNCTIONS

Innovating LeaderTypes focus attention on what could be or what might be, creatively imagining multiple possibilities from the kernel of an idea, the 'aha!' moment. They perceive patterns and interconnections across diverse contexts, 'connecting the dots' in various domains to transplant and apply concepts from one milieu to another. They are champions of the next big idea and promoters of the new-and-improved. Consider FDR's New Deal, Kennedy's New Frontier, Reagan's new direction (not an official program), and Clinton's positioning himself as a New Democrat. All share a dominant Innovating LeaderType.

If one is lucky, a solitary fantasy can totally transform one million realities. MAYA ANGELOU

An Innovating LeaderType's penchant for storyboarding and storytelling means she can envision a wide range of scenarios, plots, and potential outcomes by extrapolating trends into the future. Her instincts tell her where the potential lies, and she leverages available resources to maximum effect. Her hunches of what's around the corner help her see the seemingly unseen, and anticipate the next moves of competitors—in business, political or military engagements.

Because Innovating LeaderTypes can easily imagine different futures, they are usually the organization's preferred change leaders. Their infectious optimism ("If we can see it, we can be it.") inspires others. They rally followers around radical change by the sheer force of their personality—whether it's a push-the-envelope innovation or a break-it-even-if-it-ain't-broke revamping of a process—these early adopters were born to "boldly go where no one has gone before."

Nothing limits achievement like small thinking; nothing expands possibilities like unleashed imagination. WILLIAM ARTHUR WARD

INNOVATING LEADERTYPE STRENGTHS

- Brainstorming; involving others in developing and pitching ideas; exploring new ventures

- Envisioning long-term potential of new concepts, and how they will 'play' in the market

- Transforming a brand, reinventing a business, remaking a program, reshaping a product

- Networking across functional, organizational, and national boundaries; staying connected

- Learning: acting as enthusiastic idea sponges and life-long learners who foster learning in others

- Leading in creative 'open spaces' where they can transform collective insights into reality

No team or organization is ever the same after an Innovating LeaderType has been at the helm.

Man's mind stretched to a new idea never goes back to its original dimensions. OLIVER WENDELL HOLMES

INNOVATING LEADERTYPE STRUGGLES

- Generating too many possibilities — all equally enticing — without a way to parse them

- Having their ideas shot down by pessimists, or being pushed prematurely for closure

- Constantly adjusting their style to influence people potentially calls into question their trustworthiness

- Failing to specify critical details of a plan; not following process; not monitoring progress

- Living too much in the future; thinking too far ahead; leaving the team to deal in reality

- Procrastinating — especially when detailed, administrative or routine tasks are involved

To quote FDR himself: *The details of this job are killing me!*

AN INNOVATING LEADERTYPE IN THE WHITE HOUSE

Read on to see how an Innovating LeaderType inhabits the Oval Office, in the presidency of Franklin D. Roosevelt.

FDR: A JUST-IN-TIME INNOVATING LEADERTYPE

PUTTING OPTIMISM AND CONFIDENCE ON DISPLAY

After ten years of Prudent LeaderTypes in the White House, the contrast could not have been clearer when Franklin Delano Roosevelt came into office. His optimism and confidence stood in stark relief to the cautious approaches of Hoover and Coolidge, as his personality was diametrically opposed to theirs. It was a time when many people were hungry, not only for food, but for a new kind of leader. FDR provided the lifeboat that a generation of Americans clung to through a singularly dark period in American history. His unyielding self-confidence helped others make it from day to difficult day. And at his death, a young solider remarked, "I felt as if I knew him...I felt as if he knew me—and I felt as if he liked me." FDR's brand of leadership was a unique combination of three LeaderTypes: Innovating, Persuasive and Inclusive. That pattern resulted in a charismatic leader who was both beloved and admired.

THE INNOVATING LEADERTYPE IN THE PRESIDENCY

Declaring "The only thing we have to fear is fear itself" in his inaugural address, Roosevelt's radical departure from the staid times of the past was further revealed in his 1935 State of the Union address: "Throughout the world, *change is the order of the day*. In every nation, economic problems, long in the making, have brought crises of many kinds for which the masters of old practice and theory were unprepared. In most nations, social justice, no longer a distant ideal, has become a definite goal, and ancient Governments are beginning to heed the call. Thus, the American people do not stand alone in the world in their desire for change." This is when the Innovating LeaderType is most needed — and most effective. Jung said of this type: "The intuitive...has a keen sense of anything new and in the making. Because he is always seeking out new possibilities, stable conditions suffocate him."

Roosevelt was bringing not just a New Deal (a label he repurposed from Mark Twain's *Connecticut Yankee*) to the American people; he was reinventing the role and office of the presidency. His Innovating LeaderType was evident in an approach to governing that was both creative and experimental: his 'brain trust' brought together the best minds in the country to explore what could be done to combat the economic paralysis of the Great Depression. He kept in close touch with the mood of the people via his network of supporters around the country, and he ultimately drove through Congress new and improved programs designed to shore up the nation's economy.

Much of his success must be attributed to his personality: Supreme Court Justice Oliver Wendell Holmes called his "a second-class intellect—but a first-class temperament."

James David Barber, in his seminal work, *The Presidential Character*, describes FDR's kind of leader: "The active-positive Presidents are those who appear to have fun in the vigorous exercise of Presidential power. They seek out—even create—opportunities for action, rather than waiting for the action to come to them." Roosevelt took up the mantle of the American presidency at a time of almost unprecedented strain on the American democracy—both from within and from without. It was clear to anyone with both a sense of history and eye on the future that the well-worn paths of the past would not provide the solutions needed to jolt America out of the dark abyss of the Great Depression. In his 1933 inaugural address he stepped outside the confines of his personality type to capture the moment, saying, "Only a foolish optimist can deny the dark realities of the moment." As Roosevelt was referring to the most pressing external threat facing the country, it's clear this reflects his Proactive LeaderType—which was very strong within him. This time must have been especially trying for an Innovating LeaderType who is typically optimistic about the future.

From the moment he took office, in true Innovating LeaderType style, he envisioned a new future, and then set about making that dream a reality. Also in keeping with his Innovating LeaderType, he combined existing resources with new concepts to develop a roadmap to success. In just his first 100 days in office he created the foundation for what became known as the New Deal:

regulation and reform of the banking system, massive government spending to prime the economic pump and restart the economy, jobs programs to put people back to work, along with creation of a social services network to support those who had fallen on hard times. As testament to his emerging Take Charge LeaderType, Roosevelt worked with Congress to enact fifteen separate bills <u>in his first three months in office</u>, including a National Banking Holiday, to help markets recover from the continuing banking crisis; the Glass-Steagall Act imposing new banking regulations; the FDIC, providing federal insurance for bank deposits; the Tennessee Valley Authority, the Public Works Administration and the National Industrial Recovery Act, all designed to help get people back to work. FDR saw the changes he and Congress imposed as part of a continuum of change that defined America. "Since the beginning of our American history we have been engaged in change—in a perpetual peaceful revolution—a revolution which goes on steadily, quietly adjusting itself to changing conditions—without the concentration camp or the quicklime in the ditch," he said.

Throughout his presidency he was an innovator, employing new technology and using resources in new and different ways. His fireside chats were delivered to Americans' homes through the fledgling medium of radio, while he often used the telephone to confer with advisers and forge partnerships. In fact, a call he made on May 28, 1940 stands as one of the most important phone calls in history. That day—as Hitler's blitzkrieg was weakening Allied forces across Europe—FDR called William Knudsen, the production wizard who had risen to the presidency of General Motors, to talk about forming a public-private industrial alliance to boost production in anticipation of a war effort. It's just this kind of future-orientation that sets FDR apart as an Innovating LeaderType: he believed the future could be created, saying, "This country has a rendezvous with destiny."

Yet another example of his Innovating style was the Lend-Lease Act. Having received a letter from Winston Churchill saying England could no longer afford war supplies, and striving to maintain the appearance of neutrality (to pacify isolationists in the political landscape and uphold the Johnson Debt-Default Act), FDR crafted an analogy to creatively pitch his idea to the country: "Suppose my neighbor's home catches fire, and I have a length of garden hose four or five hundred feet away. If he can take my garden hose and connect it up with his hydrant, I may help him to put out his fire...I don't say to him before that operation, 'Neighbor, my garden hose cost me $15; you have to pay me $15 for it.'... I don't want $15 – I want my garden hose back after the fire is over." It won passage, helped England in a time of need, and presaged the United States' entry into World War II.

Of course, no leader is without challenges – and this president is no exception. Historians have noted FDR often proved a confusing, frustrating, and spotty administrator as he directed the nation's military and industrial preparations for war (Prudent being the opposite of his Innovating LeaderType). Prominent members of his cabinet and staff found all these failures exasperating. Examining this through the lens his LeaderType, it's a typical failing of an Innovating LeaderType whose constant focus on the future can impair performance in the present. Realizing this about his leadership style, he once said, "A good leader cannot get too far ahead of his followers. It's a terrible thing to look over your shoulder when you are trying to lead — and find no one there." He recognized the struggle of bringing people along with you as you forge ahead. A colleague in leadership development at a global Fortune 300 once gave the Innovating CEO this feedback: "You're like a speeding train; once in a while, you need to stop at a station, and let people get onboard." Imagine Eleanor Roosevelt giving Franklin this advice — or something similar — given his sense of urgency, and his admitted tendency to get out in front of the body politic.

HOW FDR'S LEADERTYPE WAS FORMED: AN EARLY DRIVE TOWARD FREEDOM AND CREATIVITY

Born into the old-line, patrician Roosevelt clan, the young Franklin had lots of freedom on the family's massive estate to explore and spread his wings (and yet, he yearned for more freedom in his daily schedule — an early clue). He reflected on his upbringing glowingly: "I received love and devotion that were perfect as a child." Along with exploring, his childhood involved travel, meeting people and adapting to his environment, all of which aligned with his extraversion. (The 'soil' in which he was planted naturally fertilized his personality type.) He was indulged by a doting mother: she nursed him for a year, didn't cut his hair until he was 4, and kept him in dresses until he was 6 (a fad at the time). After her husband had a heart attack (when Franklin was 8), she sought to create an idealistic, trouble-free world where only positivity was allowed for the sake of her husband. Franklin's father slowly deteriorated, becoming an invalid, passing away when FDR was 19.

Family members and caregivers have reported that from childhood FDR had an active imagination, which would later take the form of exaggeration or outright fabrication. His early sense of humor, his love of puns, gossip, and a good joke, and his frequent use of exclamation points ("my dear mama, we coasted! yesterday nothing dangerous, yet look out for tomorrow!!, your boy, F.") reveal a creative mind not bounded by reality—and one which looked ahead. His extraversion, though not as pronounced as his cousin, Theodore's, still defined him throughout his life, as he connected with people of all ranks and stations in life. Reflecting the core of his personality type, he once said, "Happiness lies not in the mere possession of money; it lies in the joy of achievement, in the thrill of creative effort."

While still in his twenties, FDR entered the political realm as a New York state senator. He had always admired the accomplishments of distant cousin Theodore, and saw in politics his chance to ply his creativity and persuasive talents to build a future for the state...and in the process, himself. That path included stints as U.S. assistant secretary of labor and governor of New York. In defining his vision of career achievement, he once said, "A man can be as great as he wants to be. If you believe in yourself and have the courage, the determination, the dedication, the competitive drive and if you are willing to sacrifice the little things in life, and pay the price for the things that are worthwhile, it can be done." These words almost sound like advice he'd received from his cousin, Theodore and repeated. He would pursue this path to the highest office in the land, despite a considerable setback, showing his courage and determination were more than just words.

Jung saw in this type the potential for possibilities to overwhelm one's judgment: "He claims a similar freedom and exemption from restraint, submitting his decisions to no rational judgment and relying entirely on his nose for the possibilities that chance throws his way." From the FDR memoirs, "Evasiveness, duplicity and underhandedness are generally taken as imperfections of character...in the case of FDR [they can be seen as] skills of a high order in the fine art of ambiguity...it is the art of keeping one's own counsel while giving others the exhilarating impression they are on the inside. In this art, FDR was peerless." Eleanor would write of her husband, "Franklin had the gift of being able to draw out the people whom he wished to draw out and to silence those with whom he was bored, and in both cases the people were greatly charmed." Herbert Hoover called him "a chameleon in plaid." FDR admitted,

> "You know I am a juggler, and I never let my right hand know what my left hand does. I may have one policy for Europe and one diametrically opposite for North and South America. I may be entirely inconsistent, and furthermore I'm perfectly willing to mislead and tell untruths if it will help win the war."

THE ULTIMATE EXAMPLE OF OPTIMISM AND WILL

The defining crisis of FDR's personal life was contracting polio at 39 (a psychologically significant time as he was being pulled towards his Proactive LeaderType at midlife), and becoming paralyzed and dependent on his wife Eleanor and son James for help. The first lady was his eyes and ears at events the often-wheelchair-bound president couldn't attend (e.g., her famous meeting with workers in a mine). And he often relied on James for (literal) support when getting in and out of his chair during public events. Eleanor's quote referring to her husband's amazing adjustment to his limitations gives insight on his approach to life generally. "Although crippled physically and prey to various infections, he was…gloriously and happily free of the various forms of psychic maladjustment which are called by such names as inhibition, complex, phobia. His mind, if not always orderly, bore no trace of paralysis and neither did his emotional constitution, and his heart was certainly in the right place." When he spoke the words "the only thing we have to fear is fear itself," people believed him; they knew he'd experienced it. LBJ said of him, "He was the only person I ever knew — anywhere — who was never afraid."

FDR'S LEADERTYPE DEVELOPS THROUGH TIME

FDR's development as a leader follows the pattern of someone with MBTI preferences for Extraversion,

Intuition, Feeling, Perceiving (ENFP). At certain ages, different aspects of his personality type came into fuller realization. These correspond to the 8 LeaderTypes showing up as follows.

- **Innovating** – From birth the driving force of his personality was his Extraverted Intuition, which Jung describes as "His capacity to inspire courage and to kindle enthusiasm for anything new is unrivalled, although he may have already dropped it by the morrow."

- **Persuasive** – In his teens he begins to display his Extraverted Feeling. This shows up in his genial nature, his socially appropriate upbringing and emphasis on positive emotions.

- **Inclusive** – In his 20s, Introverted Feeling emerges as indicated by his break with his mother in deciding to marry Eleanor, a decision reflecting his authentic feelings for her. It also shows up in his concern for those less fortunate; he was called a traitor to his class.

- **Visionary** – In his mid-30s, Introverted Intuition kicks in, as revealed by what many refer to as his 'dormant' period, but where I believe he was building his vision for his future.

Midlife crisis: late-30s/early 40s for FDR was his struggle to deal with the debilitating effects of polio, and come to terms with who he had been, and what his future might be.

- **Proactive** – In his 40s, FDR becomes hyperactive in his quest to remake himself—and those around him;

he's known as 'Dr. Roosevelt' to fellow polio patients at Warm Springs, and he's elected Governor of New York by age 47, a remarkable feat for someone physically disabled at that time in this country's history.

- **Take Charge** – By the time he takes office as president, his Extraverted Thinking has emerged, and I believe, shows itself dramatically in his driving legislation through Congress in his first 100 days. Of course, the thrust of the New Deal was more reflective of his Innovating LeaderType (the next new thing / big idea), but his Take Charge LeaderType supported it vigorously.

- **Independent** – When he was leading the war effort, this LeaderType began to emerge. His thinking clarified, and he sought to define the terms and conditions of a postwar world at Yalta.

- **Prudent** – He passed away at age 63, giving this LeaderType little time to emerge.

Franklin Delano Roosevelt shows little in the way of neuroticism according to the seven historian-experts, and excellent type development from my perspective. He was clearly twice-born, a prerequisite, I believe, to becoming a truly great leader. Did he have flaws? Of course he did. But, it's how he managed those, and overcame adversities that prove his mettle. FDR was just what the country needed at that crucial juncture: an inspiring, Innovating-Persuasive leader proclaiming "Happy Days Are Here Again."

Franklin Roosevelt – Summary Profile

Leadership positions: member, New York State Senate; assistant secretary of the navy; governor of New York; president (1933 – 1945)

Age while president: 51 – 63

LeaderTypes:

Strongest: Innovating

Supporting: Persuasive, Inclusive

Emerging: Take Charge, Independent (while president)

Weakest: Prudent

MBTI preferences (clarity):

- **Extraversion** (clear)

- **Intuition** (slight)

- **Feeling** (moderate)

- **Perceiving** (moderate)

Prominent Qualities:	Positive Emotions, Assertive, Ambitious
Prominent Deficits:	Not straightforward, Not dutiful, Not vulnerable, Not modest
Motivational need(s):	Achievement, Power
SCARF triggers:	Status, Autonomy, Fairness

COACHING THE INNOVATING LEADERTYPE IN YOU

If Innovating is <u>not</u> your dominant LeaderType, you might want to consider the following questions (these would come naturally to an Innovating leader).

- What can you imagine happening in the next few years? Where is your world headed?

- What's an idea or possibility you haven't pursued? How might you explore its potential?

- How can you spark people's imagination? How can you encourage boundary-less thinking?

- Who can you connect with — or interconnect among your connections — for strategic benefit?

- What's a concept gleaned from an unrelated field? How might you apply that to your world?

- What's a metaphor or analogy for your present situation? How does that shift your thinking?

If Innovating is your dominant LeaderType, consider these questions to challenge you further:

- What's new in your world? What's changing? What's the potential inherent in this change?

- What's one step you could take in the direction of change, or toward your perfect future?

- How do you read the corporate mood? What's your intuition telling you about the players?

- What details are you possibly overlooking? What processes/procedures are you neglecting?

- What patterns or trends do you see with regard to how you/your team got into this situation?

- If often changing style, how can you show you are consistent (e.g., your values, principles)?

- How do you bring your team along with you? How do you align them with your vision?

QUOTES FOR AN INNOVATING JOURNEY

Without this play with fantasy no creative work has ever yet come to birth. The debt we owe to the play of the imagination is incalculable. CARL JUNG

The most valuable "currency" of any organization is the initiative and creativity of its members. Every leader has the solemn moral responsibility to develop these to the maximum in all his people. This is the leader's highest priority.
W. EDWARDS DEMING

The man with a new idea is a Crank until the idea succeeds.
MARK TWAIN

The sure path to oblivion is to stay where you are.
BERNARD FAUBER

Innovation distinguishes between a leader and a follower.
STEVE JOBS

Some kind of widespread enthusiasm or excitement is apparently needed for the realization of vast and rapid change.
ERIC HOFFER

What I do best is share my enthusiasm. BILL GATES

Chapter Six:
The Visionary LeaderType Thomas Jefferson, 3rd President of the United States

THE VISIONARY BRAND: INVENTIVE DREAMER

WHEN PEOPLE WORK WITH Visionary LeaderTypes, they see their own and their leader's dreams clearly illuminated. In fact, the Visionary Leader is like a prophet who paints a portrait of what could be for his followers, works backward from that vision, and then charts a course forward. He thinks holistically, imagines future impacts, and sees big-picture possibilities.

The very essence of leadership is that you have a vision. You can't blow an uncertain trumpet.
THEODORE HESBURGH

What better example of the Visionary LeaderType than Thomas Jefferson? Long before he charged Lewis and Clark with finding a route to the Pacific, he dreamed and wrote about sending explorers across the continent.

Then, in true Visionary LeaderType fashion, he made that vision a reality. Back in the early years of the nineteenth century, there were few around him who thought the legendary explorers would ever survive the rigors of a transcontinental journey. But Jefferson trusted his vision, and created that future.

Your imagination is your preview of life's coming attractions. ALBERT EINSTEIN

HOW THE VISIONARY LEADERTYPE FUNCTIONS

How does he do it? Jung said, "It is always something that is unconscious until the moment it appears, and so presents itself as if it had fallen from heaven. The Germans call this *Einfall,* which means a thing that falls into your head from nowhere. Sometimes it is like a revelation." (*The Collected Works, Vol. 18*). Visionary LeaderTypes thus operate best where there are no established conditions or guidelines for what to think. Once the insight, inspiration, or instinctual nudge comes, he's off and running: focusing his attention on the origin, interpretation and integration of that abstract idea, image or vision. He pays close attention to his premonitions, often musing about where something came from and/or where it's going. Using pictures and symbols, he explores their potential significance today — and tomorrow. Of all possible futures, he is best able to divine where things will lead, and what the endgame will be.

We go where our vision is. JOSEPH MURPHY

You will often find the Visionary Leader reflecting on deeper meaning of current events, future states, and other pressing issues. He is a contemplative, intentional, conceptual, holistic, paradoxical, and insightful, dreamer. He thrives where he can explore novel problems, unravel mysteries, render visions, or synthesize concepts. Think of him creating elegant designs (formerly blueprints) for reaching some significant purpose. You might envision him asking the question, "What does it all mean?" often serving as the organization's resident philosopher or prophet.

Imagination is the reality of the dreamer. SCOTT RINGENBACH

VISIONARY LEADERTYPE STRENGTHS

- Instinctively trusting insights/hunches as future guides; somehow knowing what will be

- Imagining where issues will lead; anticipating/preventing likely barriers; leading in the "dark"

- Reflexively envisioning a desired outcome; insentiently following the best route to success

- Integrating complex data; seeing interconnections in seemingly unrelated material or realms

- Exploring subjects for nuanced positions; identifying systemic issues or universal themes

- Getting to the crux of the matter; seeking and deriving deeper meaning for the journey

- Assessing potential in oneself and the team; helping realize synergistic potential in situations

I prefer the dreams of the future to the history of the past. THOMAS JEFFERSON

VISIONARY LEADERTYPE STRUGGLES

- Failing to see history as a master teacher; not seeking out or incorporating lessons learned

- Absorbing new, external, incontrovertible data—especially when it contradicts their image

- Wrongly interpreting events; reading too much into things; incorrectly attributing motives

- Simplifying complexity; overcomplicating the simple; inadequately articulating their vision

- Explaining concepts to anyone who just doesn't get it; engaging in superficial conversation

- Lacking a sense of urgency, agility, or responsiveness; not grasping the immediate reality

Without vision the people perish. THE BIBLE, PROVERBS 29:18

THE VISIONARY LEADERTYPE IN THE WHITE HOUSE

For a realization of the Visionary LeaderType, see how it played out in Thomas Jefferson's life.

THOMAS JEFFERSON: AN INSCRUTABLE, VISIONARY LEADER
MAKING VISION A REALITY

Understanding Thomas Jefferson has been the subject of countless books—and the title of one—about the third president of the United States. Attempting to discover *The Real Jefferson*, biographers have plumbed the *Inner Jefferson,* with one calling the final result, *Portrait of an Enigma.* Dumas Malone, author of no less than six volumes on Jefferson, affirmed his subject was "a hard man to know intimately." Merrill Peterson, perhaps his most celebrated biographer, confessed: "Of all his great contemporaries Jefferson is perhaps the least self-revealing and the hardest to sound to the depths of being. It is a mortifying confession, but he remains for me, finally, an impenetrable man." Summed up as an *American Sphinx* and a paradoxically *Grieving Optimist* by other authors, Jefferson remains largely a mystery.

Why such mystification about the man? I believe much of the explanation lies in his personality type. Jung described introverted intuition types (Jefferson's dominant function) as "...almost inaccessible to judgment from outside...he may even become a complete enigma to his immediate circle." Among the eleven historian-specialists who assessed Jefferson's personality were widely diverging views of him on every dimension <u>except one</u>: the one that strongly correlates with a Jungian preference for intuition. This combined with his preference for introversion makes Jefferson the epitome of the Visionary LeaderType—the principal quality of which is the ability to see the future, to visualize what's around the corner, metaphorically, sometimes literally.

This type has "…a visionary idea by which he himself is shaped and determined," said Jung. Jefferson's "philosophy was cast in the future tense," said biographer Daniel Boorstin. Jefferson was compelled by his crystal-clear idea of what America should be: an agrarian-based, well-educated democratic republic of limited, decentralized government. Jefferson was America's first prophet, and his mission—carried out with Persuasive zeal—was to help the fledgling country realize its destiny. Even Jefferson saw the habits of his mind as predetermined: "Our opinions are not voluntary." This produced a unique leadership style, the essence of which was forward-looking: "I like the dreams of the future better than the history of the past," he said, believing, "History, in general, only informs us of what bad government is."

Another source of puzzlement about his personality, I believe, stems from his amazing type development: Jefferson vividly displayed all eight LeaderTypes—more so than any other president in this book. E. M. Halliday called him "Unarguably a complicated man." The philosopher and psychologist, John Dewey hailed him as the "most universal" man. Jefferson both extraverted ("much may be done if we are always doing"), and introverted ("delay is preferable to error"), with the latter his preference ("Be polite to all, but intimate with few").

Jefferson's words reflect a balance between his outer and inner worlds, the pragmatic and the intuitive, the actual and potential, and most of all, his head and his heart. He possessed incredibly detailed knowledge of multiple disciplines, and still had room in his fertile mind for wildly creative possibilities, resulting in many inventions.

His ability to hold the tension of opposites, and his capacity for fully functioning, diverse cognitive processes sets Thomas Jefferson apart. Then there is his ingenious intellect, which yielded prodigious content through those cognitive processes. Jefferson also appears to have had few emotional triggers — or if he did, he mastered them with an uncanny level of emotional intelligence. For all these capabilities, he was still very human. His public, egalitarian ideals must be juxtaposed against his private, repressive ownership of 200 people — including Sally Hemmings, with whom he fathered several children. I believe even this aspect of his life can be explained by his personality type. The unconscious (or shadow) function for someone with such a clearly introverted, intuitive preference is extraverted Sensation: deriving physical or aesthetic pleasure from sensual or adventurous experiences. Someone in the grip of that 'shadow' — even as typologically developed as he was — would be decidedly clouded in his judgment. This undercurrent of extraverted Sensation showed up in other ways: while he favored public and private frugality, he "spent lavishly on his personal comforts," (Ellis) driving himself deeply into debt. Carey McWilliams called his "a character which seems to be made up of warring antitheses." Perhaps Jefferson summed up himself best: "Of all machines, ours is the most complicated and inexplicable."

HOW JEFFERSON'S LEADERTYPE
WAS FORMED

Burstein described Thomas Jefferson as an "essentially private person" who "concealed his inner feelings behind an almost impenetrable wall of reserve." Cautious and efficient in disclosure, Jefferson once said, "The most valuable of all talents is that of never using two words when one will do." While not always an indication of introversion, Jefferson was shy. He preferred the solitude of reading, researching, and writing to social activities. His best friend in college and perhaps throughout his entire life, John Page, compared himself to Jefferson in this way, "I was too sociable, and fond of the conversation of my friends, to study as Mr. Jefferson did, who could tear himself away from his dearest friends, to fly to his studies."

Socially, young Tom Jefferson was challenged. Recounting his first meeting with Rebecca Burwell to a friend, "I had dressed up in my own mind such thoughts as occurred to me, in as moving language as I knew how, and expected to have performed them in a tolerably credible manner. But, good God! When I had an opportunity of venting them, a few broken sentences, uttered in great disorder, and interrupted with pauses of uncommon length, were the too-visible marks of my strange confusion!" While the last sentence no doubt mirrors many a 19-year-old's first love, the first sentence certainly reveals an introvert's preference to think, rehearse, and then speak.

His yearning to learn was innate: "A patient pursuit of facts, and cautious combination and comparison of them, is the drudgery to which man is subjected by his Maker, if he wishes to attain sure knowledge." (This reveals his Independent and Take Charge LeaderTypes.) Boorstin said, "The Jeffersonian was not himself disheartened by his inability to explain the connection between the common universe of man's senses (facts) and the miscellaneous product of men's brains (ideas)." And, "For by warning against abstraction, by questioning systems, and by attacking purism, the philosopher (Jefferson) saw himself bridging the gap between mind and matter, idea and experience." (Again, this reveals both Independent and Take Charge LeaderTypes.)

Copies of more than 18,000 of his letters (out of 24,000 written) still exist. He kept extraordinary records of his correspondence with friends, colleagues, even strangers, but he burned all copies of letters to his wife and to his mother. In another demonstration of his introverted preference, he gave strict do-not-disturb instructions to his staff when writing letters. This was Thomas Jefferson's way of cultivating one-on-one relationships, a practice he encouraged.

G. K. van Hogendorp, one of his younger correspondents, said of Jefferson: "He has a shyness that accompanies true worth, which is at first disturbing and which puts off those who seek to know him. Those who persist in knowing him soon discern the man of letters, the lover of natural history, law, statecraft, philosophy, and the friend of mankind." Famously bookish, Jefferson once said, "I cannot live without books." Upon hearing that his birthplace and current home, Shadwell, had burned in the War of 1812, the first thing Jefferson asked was, "Were you able to save my books?" (Sadly, none.) By the end of his life he had accumulated over 6,400 volumes—an impressive number considering he had to start from scratch after the fire. It was this personal library that he sold, at much less than replacement value, to revive the Library of Congress.

Soft-spoken (almost incapable of raising his voice), a "poor" to "mediocre" public speaker, and born when the written word ruled, Thomas Jefferson's pen was oh-so-mightier than his sword—or his vocal chords. Others looked to his leadership precisely because of what and how he wrote. His *Summary View on the Rights of British Americans* was much more a reflection of his thoughts and ideals than the subsequent *Declaration of 1776* (as it was known), the latter reflecting a consensus of American thought as Congress edited his original work by more than 400 words. It was his pointed, elegantly crafted *Summary View* that rallied protesters in Virginia and the rest of the colonies, and which certainly got the attention of King George III and the English Parliament. Interestingly, he was third in line to write the *Declaration*. Benjamin Franklin refused to write anything for others to edit, and John Adams handed the task over to him, admiring the young Virginian's unmatched articulacy and keen mind. To his dying day, Adams regretted not writing the document that defined the new nation.

Jefferson was an amazing, prolific inventor, developing: the swivel chair, the folding ladder, a folding music stand, the lazy Susan, a cipher wheel for cryptography, and a moldboard plow that he developed by observing firsthand what was needed to boost productivity in farming. One of the hallmarks of introverted intuition is the capacity to envision a new innovation, product, or building in almost blueprint detail. "Privately he was always absorbed in design and redesign..." Burstein wrote, especially where Monticello, his "well-ordered dream-world," was concerned.

Jefferson loved languages, studied Greek and Latin early, and learned French later. Although he abandoned his early love of poetry, he enjoyed novels of fiction and abstraction, his favorite author being Laurence Sterne. One of his favorite books, as described by Halliday, reveals his intuitive preference: "*Tristram Shandy* is no ponderous tale of moral edification, but an amazing collage of narrative sketches, satirical skits, mock essays, and whimsical digressions, composing a very long work that is saturated with sexual innuendo." Burstein, going further, quotes Frederick Garber who, describing *Tristram Shandy,* reveals the inner workings of an introverted intuitive: "The energies of the imagination are so fully internalized that they turn in upon themselves, use themselves as characters, and shape the narrative out of their own capacity for shaping."

A VISIONARY LEADER IN THE EXECUTIVE MANSION

Jefferson's first inaugural address gives a glimpse into his intuitive mind. Jefferson posed a rhetorical question (itself a clue) to those who doubted his vision of limited government: "Would the honest patriot, in the full tide of successful experiment, abandon a government which has so far kept us free and firm on the theoretic and visionary fear that this government, the world's best hope, may by possibility want energy to preserve itself? I trust not." This is not something a Proactive leader would likely say.

Jefferson's presidency had an audacious beginning and a troubled finish. Substantive domestic achievements were followed by an ill-conceived international initiative. By 1804, Jefferson had presided over the popular Louisiana Purchase and fulfilled his promises to shrink the federal government, reduce the national debt, and eliminate internal taxes. His intuitive sense served him well: with dubious constitutional authority he seized the opportunity inherent in Napoleon's offer to sell—before he had a chance to withdraw it. In one fell stroke he nearly doubled the size of the country, realizing his vision of an agrarian empire. His rationale, too, was right out of his personality: strategic intent with some Feeling concern: "The acquisition of Louisiana ... by giving the exclusive navigation of the Mississippi (sic), it avoids the burthens (sic) & sufferings of a war, which conflicting interests on that river would inevitably have produced." Criticized as pursuing anything but limited government whenever it suited his purpose, Jefferson facilitated what no one until then had envisioned: a continent-spanning country "from sea to shining sea."

As secretary of state in the Washington administration, Jefferson had hired a journalist to criticize the president and his policies, but denied doing so. He declared his opposition to parties, but helped found the Democratic-Republican Party. Most notably, his vision decidedly clashed with Alexander Hamilton's goal of a centralized commercial/banking federation. Jefferson was remarkably successful in devising new ways to accomplish his purposes, including personal politicking (especially at dinner parties), use of the press to his advantage, and liaisons with Congress. He was a master of declaring (and getting people to believe) his intentions—even though contrary to the results of his actions. While publicly maintaining that he did not involve himself in the business of Congress, nothing could be farther from the truth. Working indirectly, sometimes drafting legislation himself for introduction by sympathetic lawmakers, he functioned almost like a present-day lobbyist. And in private, he admitted how important it was to influence Congress, preferring not to leave the government to "chance and not of design." (Cunningham)

His political innovations likely inspired inventive acts by later presidents. His Take Charge LeaderType emerged just as he was elected, and resulted in his being an efficient administrator who did not hesitate to use all the powers he considered inherent in the office. He dispensed with Washington's ceremonies, but continued his method of delegation and consultation among the members of his staff while ensuring that final decision-making rested with him. Jefferson had strongly held convictions, but they were subject to what he could pragmatically accomplish. He could encourage Congress to prohibit the importation of slaves at the earliest permissible opportunity, 1808, but he could not compel Virginia or any other state to abolish the peculiar institution itself, nor could the federal government do so on its own authority.

Jefferson's political beliefs were more straightforward and won the day over a second term of John Adams. The election in 1800 marked the first transformation of power from one political party to another in the nation's history—all the more significant because, contrary to the Revolution in France—it occurred without violence. Although Jefferson's republicanism placed him in direct opposition to his Federalist predecessors, his Extraverted Feeling came through in his inaugural address, offering a conciliatory note: "We are all republicans: we are all federalists. If there be any among us who would wish to dissolve this Union or to change its republican form, let them stand undisturbed as monuments of the safety with which error of opinion may be tolerated where reason is left free to combat it." His words were incredibly prescient and still relevant more than 200 years later.

The Embargo of 1807 showed what happens when a Visionary leader's vision is not the correct one. Hostilities between France and England had been held in check for much of Jefferson's first term, but they broke out again early in his second term. In response to the plundering of American ships, Jefferson instituted a strict embargo on American shipping to England and France. Jefferson's intuitive sense was that if France and Britain were deprived of trade with the United States they would be forced to alter their policies. The principal effect of the embargo, however, was to close American ports, foster smuggling, and cripple the economy, particularly that of New England. Jefferson responded to efforts to evade the embargo with a policy of draconian repression (his somewhat undeveloped Extraverted Thinking emerging) that ran counter to his libertarian ideals. The embargo and Jefferson's efforts to enforce it proved as politically costly for him as the Alien and Sedition Acts had been for Adams. Jefferson, tired of the shackles of power, did not seek a third term in 1808.

BEYOND JEFFERSON'S VISIONARY LEADERTYPE

Jefferson's temperament could best be described as idealistic. His Feeling preference, in tandem with his Intuition, is reflected in this quote from a letter to Charles McPherson in 1773: "The glow of one warm thought is to me worth more than money." Another quote from a letter to Maria Cosway reflects this idealism, and focuses on the positive. "For assuredly nobody will care for him who cares for nobody. But friendship is precious not only in the shade but in the sunshine of life: and thanks to a benevolent arrangement of things, the greater part of life is sunshine."

Jefferson's development as a leader is revealed in this path:

- **Visionary** – The Louisiana Purchase was his strategic acquisition, and through the eyes of Lewis and Clark, he could see America reaching from coast-to-coast. It was, however, his vision that so conflicted with Alexander Hamilton's (of a financially centralized federation), and which, to this day, continues to be debated.

- **Inclusive** – He acknowledged the human condition; he believed in the authentic expression of one's ideas and beliefs. No matter how much he might disagree, he could respect the difference if born out of honest, human experience.

- **Persuasive** – He established multiple circles of mutual interest and like-mindedness. He wrote in a letter to Abigail Adams, "I am never happier than when I am performing good offices for good people; and the most friendly office one can perform is to make worthy characters acquainted with one another."

- **Innovating** – He "disdained conventional wisdom," (E. M. Halliday) even creating new words. He launched a country, invented political parties, and imagined and designed countless improvements for everyday life.

Midlife: His wife, Martha, died, and he promised her on her deathbed never to remarry.

- **Prudent** – He kept track of innumerable details; he disliked abstractions immensely, and in a letter to John Adams later in his life: "When once we quit the basis of sensation, all is in the wind. To talk of immaterial existences, is to talk of nothings."

- **Independent** – During this time, Jefferson was U.S. secretary of state, vice president, and not particularly effective. Obviously, his ideas had been defined and refined out of this part of his personality.

- **Take Charge** – Jefferson came into this dominating nature about the time of his inauguration, and it suited him well, in terms of administering and executing the duties of the office; however, it got out of hand with the Embargo Act of 1807. His quote that "Facts must displace theories," reveals his type progression from Independent (Introverted Thinking) to Take Charge (Extraverted Thinking).

- **Proactive** – His least-developed or 'shadow' function. This revealed itself in his lavish entertaining (going into debt as a result) and penchant for sensual experiences.

Jefferson's personality is summed up best I think in this quote by Andrew Burstein: "Just as he believed in a vision of political liberty requiring a well-ordered, broadly understood structure, Jefferson also saw friendship as a blessing built upon a universally appreciated moral foundation." His leadership legacy can be summed up in a quote from Daniel J. Boorstin: "The special philosophic mission of America for many years to come was to be the elaboration of the Jeffersonian spirit: the unhampered development of man's capacity for adaptation and adjustment, and the fruition of a society built on largely naturalistic foundations."

Thomas Jefferson was America's first Visionary leader. Though challenged personally in living up to his ideals, I submit he envisioned the day when they would be realized. And it is that idealism which continues to challenge us to fulfill his vision of "a more perfect Union."

Thomas Jefferson – Summary Profile

Leadership positions: Virginia House of Burgesses; delegate, Second Continental Congress; member, Virginia House of Delegates; governor, Virginia; commissioner/minister to France; secretary of state; vice-president; president (1801 – 1809)

Age while president: 57 – 65

LeaderTypes:

Strongest: Visionary

Supporting: Inclusive, Persuasive, Independent

Emerging: Take Charge (while president)

Weakest: Proactive

MBTI preferences (clarity):

- **Introversion** (moderate)

- **Intuition** (very clear)

- **Feeling** (moderate)

- **Judging** (moderate)

Prominent Qualities: Idealistic, Ambitious

John Q. Adams said of him, "His talents were of the highest order, his ambition transcendent, and his disposition to intrigue irrepressible."

Woodrow Wilson said of him, "The immortality of Jefferson does not lie in any of his achievements, but in his attitude toward mankind."

Prominent Deficits:	Hypocrisy/incongruity between his public views and personal life
Motivational need(s):	Power, Affiliation
SCARF triggers:	Relatedness, Fairness

COACHING THE VISIONARY LEADERTYPE IN YOU

If Visionary is <u>not</u> your dominant LeaderType, consider these suggestions and questions to help develop Visionary traits. These would come naturally to a Visionary leader.

- Via meditation or mindfulness, let go of conscious thoughts. What insights or images come?

- Look ahead. Where do you see yourself or your organization a year from now? Several years from now?

- See, imagine, or visualize your ideal future. What's happening? What's significant for you?

- Work backwards from the vision. What preceded it? What caused it? What do you infer from it?

- Look for patterns in a situation. What insights, analogies or metaphors come?

- Go to sleep with a challenge or issue on your mind. Upon waking, record your ideas.

Jung referred to Intuition as "perception via the unconscious," describing it as about understanding from whence something came, and where it was going. His early clinical practice involved word association and dream interpretation to uncover the part played by the unconscious in our psyche. Leaders need to pay much more attention to their spontaneous insights, hunches and 'aha!' moments, asking themselves where did that come from? What does it mean? Where could it take me/us?

If Visionary is your dominant LeaderType, consider these questions to further challenge you.

- When and how do insights present themselves? How can you recreate those conditions?

- How might you synthesize inputs to describe the essence of a challenge in its simplest form?

- How might you be overcomplicating a dilemma? How might you solve your Gordian knot?

- When have intuitions gotten you into trouble or gotten the best of you? How might you prevent that?

- Are you aware of interpreting others' motives? How might you be projecting onto situations?

- What filter or judgment do you need to employ to check and balance your intuitive insights?

QUOTES FOR A VISIONARY JOURNEY

I dream for a living. STEVEN SPIELBERG

Nothing happens unless first a dream. CARL SANDBURG

Imagination is more important than knowledge. For knowledge is limited, whereas imagination embraces the entire world, stimulating progress, giving birth to evolution.
ALBERT EINSTEIN

Business, more than any other occupation, is a continual dealing with the future; it is a continual calculation, an instinctive exercise in foresight. HENRY R. LUCE

Always design a thing by considering it in its next larger context — a chair in a room, a room in a house, a house in an environment, an environment in a city plan. ELIEL SAARINEN

I am a physicist who studies crystals, patterns and symmetry. So I am looking across different fields for similarities: physics, sociology, social sciences, Chinese philosophy... PETER LOLY, THE MAGNIFICENT 16, DANIELLE POIRIER, EDITOR

Visionary people are visionary partly because of the very great many things they do not see. BERKELEY RICE

I do not believe that I am now dreaming, but I cannot prove that I am not. BERTRAND RUSSELL

Section III
The Third Element of Leadership: Engage Commitment

Leadership is influence. JOHN C. MAXWELL

HOW A LEADER SEEKS, secures, and sustains the full and willing commitment of followers is the third Element of Leadership. Before a leader can Drive Performance (the fourth Element), she must Engage Commitment—otherwise it's compliance, and compliance does not equal Commitment. What is involved is no less than full and transparent disclosure with individuals on the team about what the journey will require—in very explicit terms.

Leadership implies followership. Mark Twain said, "He who leads, when no one follows, is just taking a walk." This symbiotic relationship must be acknowledged, built, nurtured, and rewarded. The dependency of leaders on followers, and followers on leaders, is absolutely essential to grasp. Who do you think is going to accomplish your ends? The skills needed are building rapport, engaging in dialogue, inviting debate, listening, building consensus, and securing agreement. This is when and how influence is brought to bear on stakeholders, customers, suppliers, partners, and employees; it's also where you and your team hold firmly to the nonnegotiable values needed to succeed.

What follows are two master examples of engaging commitment, one introverted (Abraham Lincoln), and the other, extraverted (Harry Truman). In an Inclusive and Persuasive way, these leaders show us how to Engage Commitment, the third Element of Leadership.

Chapter Seven:
The Inclusive LeaderType
Abraham Lincoln, 15th
President of the United States

THE INCLUSIVE BRAND: INSIDE-OUT
TEAM BUILDER

NEED A COMPASSIONATE, EMPATHETIC leader? Look to an Inclusive LeaderType. That's where you'll find a repository of kindness, concern, fairness, and respect. The Inclusive LeaderType will always hold fast to a set of internal values, seeking both internal and external harmony. Their respect for others makes them trustworthy leaders and reliable team players.

> *He is greatest whose strength carries up the most hearts by the attraction of his own.*
> HENRY WARD BEECHER

Many historians have held up President Abraham Lincoln as an example of inclusive leadership. Doris Kearns Goodwin in her 2005 bestseller, *Team of Rivals: The Political Genius of Abraham Lincoln,* looks at the leader's remarkable cabinet, composed of political luminaries from opposing political parties. Despite his cabinet members' different affiliations, they worked together as a team through a period of unprecedented national stress. It was Lincoln's strong hand and coalescing spirit that created the atmosphere of unity and teamwork.

> *Servant-leadership is more than a concept, it is a fact. Any great leader, by which I also mean an ethical leader of any group, will see herself or himself as a servant of that group and will act accordingly.*
> M. Scott Peck

HOW THE INCLUSIVE LEADERTYPE FUNCTIONS

Inclusive LeaderTypes will always work to respect, value, and include all, while at the same time hoping to satisfy their own need to feel respected, valued, and included. They will generally try to reach conclusions based on harmony with their personal, often nonnegotiable, values. They believe that adherence to a set of moral values is what's most important in any situation or endeavor. Inevitably, the Inclusive LeaderType searches for the good in people, always wanting to believe the best.

> *I keep my ideals, because in spite of everything I still believe that people are really good at heart.*
> Anne Frank

In any organization, the Inclusive LeaderType will seek out opportunities to bring people together, always serving as a unifying force. They are the ultimate team players and leaders, fostering an atmosphere that emphasizes harmony and fairness.

Things that matter most must never be at the mercy of things that matter least.
JOHANN WOLFGANG VON GOETHE

INCLUSIVE LEADERTYPE STRENGTHS

- Identifying what matters most in accomplishing the group's vision, mission, and goals
- Ensuring individuals and organizations stay true to their stated core beliefs and values
- Appraising and guarding individual/team values, congruence between words and actions
- Valuing, including people; supporting individuals/the team often in self-sacrificing way
- Actively listening; understanding people in-depth; remembering little things, or themes
- Expressing sincere appreciation for the person, and the individual's efforts, potential and contributions
- Displaying unique self-awareness regarding personal truth, values and meaning in life

INCLUSIVE LEADERTYPE STRUGGLES

- Others' lack of understanding, trust, respect, transparency, congruence or authenticity
- Dealing with performance issues; having to deliver or receive candid, corrective feedback

- Asserting own position/interests; standing firm under pressure; accommodating too easily
- Avoiding the instigation of healthy conflict, or striving to maintain harmony at all costs
- Competing (when necessary) in a way that honors inherent value of all, even competitors
- Setting clear goals and expectations; delegating or holding employees firmly accountable

People don't mind being challenged to do better if they know the request is coming from a caring heart.
KEN BLANCHARD

AN INCLUSIVE LEADERTYPE IN THE WHITE HOUSE

To see an Inclusive LeaderType at work in the White House, read the following profile of President Abraham Lincoln who said, "I find mercy bears richer fruits than strict justice."

ABRAHAM LINCOLN: THE INCLUSIVE LEADERTYPE
SHAPING THE AMERICAN CHARACTER

Where to begin assessing the leadership of perhaps the greatest of all U.S. presidents?

- With his character? If Heraclitus was right—that "character is destiny"—Abraham Lincoln's morality shaped the United States' character and its destiny.

- With his brilliant mind? A literary genius despite only one year of schooling, and the only president to hold a patent (Jefferson's inventions came before there was a U.S. Patent Office), Lincoln trained his powerful intellect on solving the country's greatest constitutional crisis, and resolved it successfully.

- With his self-acknowledged ambition? His desire to be remembered for doing something great, coupled with nonstop self-education and self-improvement ("Whatever you are, be a good one."), garnered him the highest office in the land — against all odds.

- With his bulldogged tenacity? Lincoln persevered through hundreds of thousands of casualties when everyone about him wanted him to give up or give in. His resolve is even more amazing given his moral objections to war.

- With his demeanor? Amiable, magnanimous, self-deprecating and folksy, Lincoln drew people to him like bees to honey, so much so that former enemies wept for days on his death. Speaker of the House Schuyler Colfax extolled his incredibly unique gift: "No man clothed with such vast power ever wielded it more tenderly and forbearingly."

THE SECRET TO HIS GREATNESS IN HIS LEADERTYPE

The qualities above would be impressive in one person. The fact that Abraham Lincoln possessed them all is nothing short of extraordinary. It would be very easy to project superhuman qualities onto "Honest Abe" (ironically,

he disliked this shortened version of his name), especially given how easy it was for history to turn him into a
martyr (given the fact he was shot on Good Friday). But
as exemplary as the above qualities are, I believe there is
a much more human answer: the key to Lincoln's greatness *can be found in his LeaderType.* **The essence of his
leadership was empathy, inclusion, and authenticity —
hallmarks of an Inclusive leader.**

Lincoln demonstrated radical inclusion on three separate, significant fronts: the nation, society at large, and
with his leadership team. On a national level, as com-
mander-in-chief, his oft stated and overarching mission
was to preserve the Union — to be inclusive toward the
South, even if it wished to be excluded. While strongly
inclusionary, he stood by his core principles. He was
unwilling to accept the southern states' secession, believing it was an act of treason. "Important principles may
and must be inflexible," he said, believing the only way
to save the country was to "resist force, employed for its
destruction, by force, for its preservation." Everything
Lincoln did as president served his all-inclusive belief in
'We the people.'

On a societal level, Lincoln was determined to bring
about inclusion of all races in defining what it meant to
be human. His long-standing, fundamental belief was
that, "If slavery is not wrong, nothing is wrong." This
led him to push the Emancipation Proclamation and gain
passage of the 13th Amendment banning slavery, building on the 1808 law banning importation of African-
American slaves. Admittedly, Lincoln's beliefs evolved.
Early speeches reveal superiority toward blacks, and

some misguided notions, most notably reparations for and the resettlement of slaves. As progressive for his time as he was, his case against slavery emerged over time. He fundamentally believed African-Americans should participate in the American dream. This shows him to be an inclusive thinker for his time. He once said, "Those who deny freedom to others, deserve it not for themselves; and, under a just God, cannot long retain it." Again, his appraisal of 'justice for all' shows the essential focus of an Inclusive leader: an internal morality that guides all decisions.

Finally, even he admitted, as humble as he was: "I may not have made as great a President as some other man, but I believe I have kept these discordant elements together as well as anyone could." Perhaps his greatest test of leadership — and evidence of inclusion — was his own cabinet. As revealed in Doris Kearns-Goodwin's *Team of Rivals,* Lincoln had to hold together coalitions, court political enemies, manage contentious factions, deal with team members operating behind his back, and stroke some very strong egos to achieve his ends. Why? He knew that if his mission were to succeed, he needed the best and brightest on his team — regardless of whether they disagreed with him or even disrespected him. I believe this level of inclusion was radical and unprecedented, and is rare even today in leadership teams at major corporations, institutions and in government. Lincoln exemplified the advice, "Keep your friends close, but your enemies closer" long before Mario Puzo penned *The Godfather* and his advice.

INCLUSION AS THE BALM FOR "THE THREAT FROM WITHIN"

Consider his accomplishments. By the time Lincoln was assassinated, barely four years after his first inauguration, a race of people was freed; the Civil War was won; the Union preserved; the Constitution reasserted; and his cabinet united in their devotion to his cause. They literally wept at his passing. At the core of these events was Lincoln's Inclusive leadership, which enabled the nation to conquer the greatest challenge to its existence until then — the threat from within.

Even before Lincoln took office the situation had deteriorated terribly, irreversibly it seemed: James Buchanan, the previous occupant of the White House, had left Washington proclaiming himself "the last President of the United States." Seven states had already seceded from the Union. Ten days before he was sworn in, Jefferson Davis was sworn in as president of the Confederate States of America. In fact, Lincoln had to be smuggled into Washington — surrounded by slave states — for his inauguration. The South had taken control of all federal agencies within its territory, and had seized almost every arsenal or fort, including those that controlled the Mississippi River. The city of Washington had little defense, and the North was completely unprepared for war. Elected with only 39.8 percent of the popular vote, Lincoln was seen by most as utterly unequal to the task. *The New York Times*, generously, called him "peculiar." But the magnitude of the task before him did not deter him. "The probability that we may fail in the struggle ought not to deter us from the support of a cause we believe to be just," he said.

In his first inaugural address, Lincoln offered — with genuine intent — an olive branch to the South:

> "We are not enemies, but friends. We must not be enemies. Though passion may have strained, it must not break the bonds of affection. The mystic chords of memory, stretching from every battlefield, and patriot grave, to every living heart and hearthstone, all over this broad land, will yet swell the chorus of Union, when again touched, as surely as they will be by the better angels of our nature."

Unfortunately, it was not received as intended in Charleston — or the rest of the South. It was perceived as a declaration of war, showing that even with noblest intent and the greatest of communication skills, Inclusive leaders can fail to bridge a gaping, trust-broken relationship. It was likely a sad realization for Lincoln that his hopes, beliefs and values were not shared, and yet he resolved to "preserve, protect and defend" the Constitution with all his heart, with his entire mind, and with all his strength.

HOW HIS PERSONALITY WAS SHAPED

Born dirt poor (in a one-room log cabin with a dirt floor), Lincoln himself summed up his early life with a quote from Thomas Gray's *Elegy Written in a Country Churchyard*: "The short and simple annals of the poor." Although his mother died when he was 9, Lincoln acknowledged her impact: "God bless my mother; all that I am or even hope to be I owe to her." Abraham dutifully handed over 100 percent of his wages to his father until the age of 21. John Romaine, one of his employers said, "He worked for me, but was always reading and thinking. I used to get mad at him for it. I'd say he was awful lazy. He would laugh and talk, crack jokes and tell stories all the time... He said to me...that his father taught him to work but never taught him to love it." He was very much a loner, in the fields and forests of the frontier, and preferred that solitude. "Silence," Carl Sandburg wrote, "found him for her own. In the making of him, the element of silence was immense."

The time in Indiana he called "pretty pinching times." His father remarried Sarah Bush Johnston, a widow whom Abraham would call "Mama" and later, his "best friend in this whole world." She would say, "His mind and mine — what little I had — seemed to run together." She defended his bookish ways to Abraham's father and nurtured his intellect. From his stepmother's point of view, Abraham was "a model child who never needed a cross word." He spent a day with his stepmother before he went to Washington in 1861, never to see her again. He had an estranged relationship with his father — and with his own eldest son, Robert. His father had grown up without any education, and perhaps was threatened by his son's intellectual capacity and ambition. At any rate, Abraham did not attend his father's funeral. When informed he was near death, Lincoln told his stepbrother "Say to him that if we could meet now, it is doubtful whether it would not be more painful than pleasant..."

Lincoln was teased as a youth — especially by girls — for his looks. He hid his hurt and shyness as a result of these taunts by playing the clown. He only began to read at age 15, when he received at most a year of education, but once he did, he was consumed with Voltaire, Paine, the Constitution and Shakespeare (*Macbeth* was his favorite).

He never apprenticed in a law firm as most did, he just read. He studied for and was admitted to the bar at age 27 — without attending law school — or any college for that matter. His self-education is a testament to the curiosity and will of a born learner.

THE INCLUSIVE LEADERTYPE ON DISPLAY

Early in his political career, support for the young Lincoln often crossed party lines. While he was affiliated with the Whig party, Democratic President Andrew Jackson appointed him postmaster of New Salem, Illinois. When he ran for the state legislature in 1834, even Democrats supported him. From early in life, Lincoln earned respect across boundaries, and learned to work collaboratively. He shared successes, and willingly accepted blame when things went wrong. He was incredibly magnanimous — even when subordinates defiantly disobeyed, disrespected or disagreed with him.

In office, Lincoln surrounded himself with people — including rivals — who had strong egos and high ambitions, who felt free to question his authority, and who were unafraid to argue with him.

For example, Lincoln brought Salmon Chase into his cabinet as treasury secretary and kept him there for three years, even though Chase craved the presidency and was undermining him. Lincoln felt that as long as he was competently fulfilling his post that was more important than his enmity towards Lincoln. Lincoln was a master at zeroing in on personality types that complemented his own. For example, his Secretary of War, Edwin Stanton, tended to be less flexible and more secretive than his superior. The two personality types effectively balanced each other. Even when appointing generals, Lincoln was blind to party affiliation; he was only concerned with a general's ability to win battles and shorten the war. Despite heavy losses at Shiloh, Lincoln appraised Grant as extremely valuable: "I can't spare him. He fights!"

An example of his ability to compromise and smooth over disagreements was his ability to calm the waters of his marriage to Mary Todd Lincoln, who history tells us was a difficult personality. An unfortunate aspect of his conflict-avoidance was his difficulty dealing with non-performance—most notably among his generals. Lincoln could not bring himself to fire or even demote leaders of his army when they weren't achieving the ends he expected in the ways he expected. He went through several before finally elevating Grant to the top job.

THE BALANCE IN HIS PERSONALITY: AUTHENTIC INTERIOR, CREATIVE EXTERIOR

Lincoln's personality shows an incredible balance—not only of extraversion and introversion, but perceiving and judging. His preference was clearly for introversion: There is not one instance of his extemporizing when giving a speech; his remarks were always carefully considered to reflect how his inner thoughts matched the audience and situation. Early solitude in the fields and forests of Kentucky and Indiana reflect this, as do his bookish pursuits. And while his profession as a lawyer certainly required logical reasoning (Thinking), which he honed considerably, it could never equal his natural preference for Feeling. The dominant force of his personality was Introverted Feeling. Many quotes reveal this, however here is one that should resonate with Inclusive LeaderTypes: "I desire so to conduct the affairs of this administration that if at the end, when I come to lay down the reins of power, I have lost every other friend on earth, I shall at least have one friend left, and that friend shall be down inside me."

Lincoln's life makes the case that trust is built from the inside out. He was at home with himself. Deep within was a self-awareness and self-acceptance that enabled him to be authentic. His incredible convictions about the human experience emanated from the core of his being and his own humble beginnings. His empathy naturally flowed to the poor, the oppressed, the illiterate, and the wounded. His character is rated among the highest of any U.S. President. Robert E. Lee, general of the Confederacy, even admitted, "I surrendered as much to Lincoln's goodness as I did to Grant's armies."

Inclusive leaders often value authenticity above all else. Lincoln desperately wanted — and argued — that the United States should be authentic to its ideals. Listen to his argument, and remedy, if he couldn't live in a country that was true to itself:

> "As a nation, we began by declaring, "All men are created equal." We now practically read it, 'All men are created equal, except Negroes.' When the Know-Nothings get control, it will read, 'All men are created equal, except Negroes, and foreigners, and Catholics.' When it comes to this I should

prefer emigrating to some other country where they make no pretense of loving liberty—to Russia, for instance, where despotism can be taken pure, without the base alloy of hypocrisy."

If there is any doubt, Lincoln summarized the essence of the Civil War: "The precise fact on which depends this controversy, (is) namely slavery, and the different views the Republicans had versus the southerners." He further stated, "Let us have faith that right makes might, and in that faith, let us, to the end dare to do our duty as we understand it." This highlights what is for the Inclusive LeaderType their ultimate source of resolve in leadership: that they are bound by what they see as morally right, and that underpins their non-negotiable values.

It was on Lincoln's exterior where we see his wooing. He learned early on in his political career—and through practicing law—how to influence others through stirring speeches with poetry, as well as literary and biblical references. Lincoln's likability should not be underestimated. Among the many reasons people liked him were his authenticity, compassion, humility, and humor. He was especially sensitive to the corrupting influence of power on people and their relationships: "Nearly all men can stand adversity, but if you want to test a man's character, give him power." Lincoln won over people by his easy accessibility, and his building of rapport, turning acquaintances into loyal followers. Using techniques straight out of influencing texts of today, he would seek something in common, relate a story of shared experience or just listen intently to what the other party had to say, and then would proceed to bring them around to his point of view. Lincoln summarized his intent and his technique thusly: "I destroy my enemies when I make them my friends." He was a man of remarkable insight, eloquence and influence, but also quite paradoxical.

- For someone who personally avoided conflict (with his wife and his generals), he commanded a war that claimed 620,000 lives—the bloodiest in U.S. history.
- Despite his very inclusive nature, his relationships with his father and with his oldest son, Robert, were the most strained and distant.
- For all his moral depth, he was a shamelessly shrewd politician—almost Machiavellian in his ends-justifies-the-means approach to governing.

The extraverted side of his personality was creative, imaginative, storytelling and incredibly intuitive about people; this was his Innovating LeaderType. Lincoln 'innovated' when it came to suspending the writ of habeas corpus (that protected citizens from search) and other laws by which he stretched the Constitution to serve his ultimate aim of preserving and protecting the Republic. "The dogmas of the quiet past are inadequate to the stormy present. The occasion is piled high with difficulty, and we must rise with the occasion. As our case is new, so we must think anew and act anew," he argued.

His Extraverted Intuition can be seen in his opportunist outlook, as those familiar with him called him a "wild, harum-scarum kind of man who always had his mind on the main chance." He was very casual (greeting White House visitors with a 'howdy' in stocking feet) and disorderly (sticking papers in his stovepipe hat). His extraverted Perceiving is also hinted at in this quote, "I claim not to have controlled events, but confess plainly that events have controlled me." He also reveals an Extraverted Intuition preference in this quote: "Now, my man, go away, go away! I cannot meddle in your case. I could as easily bail out the Potomac River with a tea-spoon as attend to all the details of the army."

One sign of emotional intelligence was his ability to let go of slights, never holding grudges. "I shall do noth-ing in malice. What I deal with is too vast for malicious dealing," he said. Lincoln received volumes of hate mail, including death warrants with rewards of $100,000. Lincoln dismissed such differences as more about the senders than it was about him. He could be very strong when what mattered most was put at the mercy of what mattered least. When slighted he never seemed to mind, thus not triggered by Status, nor it would seem, trig-gered by Certainty, Autonomy, or Relatedness—in fact, he saw the world as we, there was no room for "us ver-sus them." But he was very triggered by Fairness. During the 1858 debates with Douglas he said, "Whenever I hear any one arguing for slavery I feel a strong impulse to see it tried on him personally.

Using his own words, Lincoln was himself the "better angel of our natures." He exemplified what we often only aspire to. His morals became the country's. His ideals about the inherent worth in every person challenged us to be better, hope more and achieve so much more than we would have without him. He led us through the dark-est depths of our history. By the sheer force of his will and his radically Inclusive nature, he held us together when we were tearing ourselves apart. It was sadly in his premature death that a groundswell of love, admiration and gratitude flowed—not only from Northerners, but also eventually from the whole country, and the rest of the world. His challenge to us is that we live up to the "better angels of our natures."

Abraham Lincoln – Summary Profile

Leadership positions: member, Illinois General Assembly; U.S. congressman; president (1861 – 1865)

Age while president: 52 – 56

LeaderTypes:

Strongest: Inclusive
Supporting: Visionary, Innovating, Persuasive
Emerging: Proactive (while president)
Weakest: Take Charge

MBTI Preferences (clarity):

- **Introversion** (moderate)
- **Intuition** (clear)
- **Feeling** (clear)
- **Perceiving** (clear)

Prominent Qualities:	Assertiveness, Trustworthiness, Character
Prominent Deficits:	Depression, Anxiety, Not straightforward
Motivational need(s):	Achievement, Affiliation
SCARF trigger(s):	Fairness

COACHING THE INCLUSIVE LEADERTYPE IN YOU

If Inclusive is <u>not</u> your dominant LeaderType, consider these questions to help develop that LeaderType. They would come naturally to an Inclusive leader.

- How does your conscience inform your leadership? What matters most to you in leading?

- How satisfied are you with how you are living your values? How can you stay true to them?

- Under what circumstances are your values most challenged? How do you protect them?

- How and with whom do you share your values? How to let them know one has been crossed?

- How important to you is being authentic and transparent? How can you manifest these more?

- How do you fully understand and empathize with someone, without projecting your feelings?

Jung said this type "is generally misunderstood...It strives after inner intensity, for which the (outer) objects serve at most as a stimulus. The depth of this feeling can only be guessed—it can never be clearly grasped." He further describes this type with the metaphor, still waters run deep. A key challenge for the Inclusive LeaderType is to be heard, to be understood and to be respected—and when not feeling heard, understood or respected—how to deal with that.

If Inclusive is your dominant LeaderType, consider these questions to challenge you.

- From where do you derive your values and beliefs? On how firm a foundation do you lead?

- How do you ensure being heard? How is your 'voice' perceived? How do you gain respect?

- How often do you use the word 'should'? How do you stay firm without being a moralizer?

- How do you keep from playing the victim in situations? How can you empower yourself?

- How might your idealism about people keep you from judging their performance accurately?

- How do you make sure you don't always accommodate for the sake of group harmony?

- Are you aware of any resentment, anger and/or shame that may skew your perception of others?

- How do you deal with these emotions? What can you do to see situations more objectively?

QUOTES FOR AN INCLUSIVE JOURNEY

We distrust our heart too much, and our head not enough. JOSEPH ROUX

With compassion, we see benevolently our human condition and the condition of our fellow beings. We drop prejudice. We withhold judgment. CHRISTINA BALDWIN

The ethic of Reverence for Life is the ethic of Love widened into universality. ALBERT SCHWEITZER

Do not worry about what others are doing! Each of us should turn the searchlight inward and purify his or her own heart as much as possible. MAHATMA GANDHI

Show me the business man or institution not guided by sentiment and service, by the idea that "he profits most who serves best," and I will show you a man or an outfit that is dead or dying. B. F. HARRIS

Everybody can be great because anybody can serve. You don't have to have a college degree to serve. You don't have to make your subject and verb agree to serve. You only need a heart full of grace. A soul generated by love. MARTIN LUTHER KING, JR.

They may forget what you said, they may forget what you did, but they will never forget how you made them feel.
CARL W. BUECHER

Chapter Eight:
The Persuasive LeaderType Harry S Truman, 33rd President of the United States

THE PERSUASIVE BRAND: HARMONIZING COLLABORATOR

THINK OF THE PERSUASIVE LeaderType as someone who knows how to get people to "yes." Through a process of engagement, dialogue, influence and mobilization, the Persuasive LeaderType is adept at bringing people around to his way of thinking. While striving to win others' commitment, he can be so diplomatic and tactful, so warm and collegial, so cooperative and harmonizing that the person being won over may be unaware of his charms.

Would you persuade, speak of Interest, not of Reason. BENJAMIN FRANKLIN

One president who understood the need to persuade was Harry Truman. He learned that, considering the amazing breadth of the modern U.S. government, a president

couldn't just make commands and expect absolute obe-
dience. He knew that various levels of government have
their own leadership structures and priorities; he saw
that the president is just one person and needs others
to get things done. He used his innate ability to bargain
and persuade others that what he wanted was in their
best interest. In commenting on President Eisenhower's
election he said, "He'll sit there all day saying do this, do
that, and nothing will happen. Poor Ike, it won't be a bit
like the military. He'll find it very frustrating."

*A leader is someone who has the ability to get other peo-
ple to do what they don't want to do, and like it.*
HARRY TRUMAN

HOW THE PERSUASIVE LEADERTYPE FUNCTIONS

The Persuasive LeaderType works to influence others
by appealing to common values. He establishes norms
and standards of acceptable behavior, and evaluates and
makes decisions based on agreement, appropriateness,
or impact on group harmony.

The Persuasive LeaderType always tries to speak and
act according to the group's values or ideals, and seeks
ways to be socially responsible. He communicates with
and relates to people to influence them in supportive,
constructive and affirming ways. Generally, he works to
maintain a positive, friendly, personally satisfying atmosphere. When a Persuasive LeaderType is in charge the
organization comes under an umbrella of protection and
care, knowing the loyalty is there for them, which in turn,

builds team spirit. Team members learn from his example that "you get more flies with honey than vinegar."

Nothing else can quite substitute for a few well-chosen, well-timed, sincere words of praise. They're absolutely free and worth a fortune. SAM WALTON

PERSUASIVE LEADERTYPE STRENGTHS

- Demonstrating warmth, concern, protection, respect for, and loyalty to team members
- Engaging and encouraging people; seeking mutual benefit in collaboration toward goals
- Influencing people and mobilizing groups — especially toward shared ideals or norms
- Fostering team spirit; helping realize team and organizational wins; aligning behaviors
- Building trust in relationships: customer, employee, supplier, shareholder, and stakeholder
- Finding common ground to foster alliances/partnerships, or in mediating opposing parties
- Providing attentive, personalized service; shaping and selling customer-oriented solutions

To be agreeable while disagreeing — that's an art. MALCOLM S. FORBES

PERSUASIVE LEADERTYPE STRUGGLES

- Dealing directly with conflict, distrust or disapproval of colleagues or team members
- Confronting those with whom they disagree in a clear, objective, nonpersonal way
- Dealing with incompetence or nonperformance; giving or receiving negative feedback
- Being 'too nice' or 'politically correct'; playing the diplomat when candor is needed
- Failing to set sufficiently aggressive goals or targets; not wanting to dampen enthusiasm
- Responding to others' questions about their motives, trustworthiness, or treasured values

The way to develop the best that is in a person is by appreciation and encouragement. CHARLES SCHWAB

THE PERSUASIVE LEADERTYPE IN THE WHITE HOUSE

Take a look at the following profile of President Harry S. Truman for an example of how a Persuasive LeaderType operates in the Oval Office.

HARRY TRUMAN: THE PERSUASIVE LEADER

BRINGING OTHERS AROUND TO HIS WAY OF THINKING

Harry S (Interestingly his middle initial did not stand for anything; it was simply the letter 'S') Truman literally defined leadership, almost from the beginning of his life until the end. And he defined leadership—whether as a military leader, judge, or president—through the lens of his Persuasive LeaderType. As far as he was concerned, leadership was all about determining and sticking to a course of action, then using whatever means at his disposal—usually with a measure of charm—to bring others around to his way of thinking. He once stated, "Do you know what makes a leader? It's a man or woman who can persuade people to do what they ought to do—and which they sometimes don't do—without being persuaded. They must also have the ability to persuade people to do what they do not want to do and like it. That, in my opinion, is the best definition of leadership."

Truman practiced the persuasion he preached. He once described the president as "...a glorified public-relations man who spends his time flattering, kissing, and kicking people..." Despite the tongue-in-cheek job description, and his uncomplicated, yet not very charismatic style, Harry Truman is one of the top ten U.S. presidents largely because of the incredible accomplishments during his presidency. Imagine the persuasion required in each of these cases.

- He sponsored the Marshall Plan to help rebuild Western Europe and head off political crisis; Truman persuaded others that it would "...go down in history as one of the greatest contributions to peace in the world."

- He contained Soviet domination of Eastern Europe after Allied portions of Berlin were blockaded, and he avoided conflict by sending supplies to the war-ravaged city via the Berlin Airlift—the beginnings of the North Atlantic Treaty Organization (NATO).

- He sent aid to Turkey and Greece to help put down Communist insurgencies, resulting in the Truman Doctrine: "I believe it must be the policy of the United States to support free people who are resisting attempted subjugation by armed minorities or by outside pressures."

- He signed the United Nations charter as a "solid structure upon which we can build a better world," and then got the Senate to ratify the treaty within a month, by a vote of eighty-nine to two.

- He sponsored creation of the state of Israel, and recognized its statehood on the day it became a nation.

- He convinced the UN to intervene in Korea—the first time the world body acted to confront an aggressor.

- He submitted to Congress the first comprehensive civil rights program proposed by a U.S. president, which included a voting rights measure. Even though Congress refused to touch it, he signed an executive order desegregating the armed forces.

Besides requiring influence and persuasion, these achievements had something else in common: they were about helping people—especially oppressed people. Summarizing what he understood his job to be, Truman said, "The very fact that he's the chief executive makes it necessary for the president to understand the nation, its relations with other nations, and its relations to the people here at home."

People had been central to his life from way back. As one local said of him, "Truman was surrounded by people, people, people." That people orientation continued throughout his life, and was evident in his feelings about politics. "If you don't like people, you hadn't ought to be in politics at all," said Truman. His fundamental job, as he saw it, was to understand people, build relationships, and protect human and civil rights: "As President of the United States, I am guided by this simple formula: to do in all cases, from day to day…what seems to me to be best for the welfare of all our people."

His persuasion naturally derived from his Extraverted Feeling. This function of his personality was expressed through respect for people, rapport and trust he built with each person, and the dialogue he had with them. It also involved considerable listening, pleading, cajoling, convincing and/or collaborating to reach a mutually beneficial solution. For a Persuasive LeaderType the litmus test is at the end of a negotiation, both parties feel the process and outcome were fair. Truman reflected this sentiment in the following quote: "It has been my experience in public life that there are few problems that cannot be worked out, if we make a real effort to understand the other fellow's point of view, and if we try to find a solution on the basis of give-and-take, of fairness to both sides."

His belief in and defense of democracy was not only learned through life experiences; I believe it coincided with and was reinforced by his Feeling preference, revealed in this quote: "Any denial of human rights is a denial of the basic beliefs of democracy." Jung said the feelings of this type (Extraverted Feeling) "harmonize with objective situations and general values…everything that fits in with objective values is good, and is loved, and everything else seems to exist in a world apart." His ideals about his country were very much tied to his personal faith: "Democracy is a matter of faith—a faith in the soul of man, a faith in human rights… Faith gives value to all things. Without faith, the people perish."

To really understand how Truman developed this philosophy and view of leadership—and became such a great leader of the Persuasive type—it's best to go back to his formative years in Missouri.

EXTRAVERTED FEELING DEVELOPS EARLY IN LIFE

In his seminal biography, *Truman,* David McCullough recounts the following vignette to show how Truman's personality was shaped at an early age: "Caroline Simpson (the maid in the Truman household) taught Harry to cook on the big wood stove and talked to him by the hour. He liked the warmth and chatter of the kitchen, liked to look after his little sister. He would sit with her in a rocking chair for hours at a time, braiding her hair or singing her to sleep. No one was ever so nice to her as her brother Harry, Mary Jane would say in later years."

For a small boy he was abnormally neat and clean. He was never popular like the other boys, never one of the "fighters" as he called them. Reminiscing years later, he spoke of the teasing he endured because of his glasses (with very thick lens): "To tell the truth, I was kind of a sissy." Still, he had found he could get most anything he wanted if he could only talk to people. In the family, Harry alone, seemed able to get along with everyone. He was the one person they could all talk to, the family peacemaker. This strongly suggests a preference for Extraverted Feeling. Often men will take an overly aggressive posture to repress their Feeling preference—for fear of being perceived as weak. Truman didn't run from that aspect of his personality; in fact, he likened himself to Abraham Lincoln in this respect.

While Truman called being a child a "very lonely thing" and claimed he had to overcome shyness, his energy from an early age was clearly directed outward—to the external world of people and events. Hometown locals described him as "always bustling around getting things done." He was unfailingly polite, and practiced piano two hours a day. He was the kid other mothers would ask their children about: "Why can't you be more like Harry Truman?" (Which didn't help make him 'one of the boys'.)

In his early years, his extraversion was visible in how he learned to deal with his world and trust that capacity: "When I was growing up it occurred to me to watch the people around me to find out what they thought and what pleased them most…I used to watch my father and mother closely to learn what I could do to please them, just as I did with my schoolteachers and playmates." According to McCullough, "He knew he had a gift for conversation. He had found he could get most anything he wanted if he could only talk to people."

BEYOND HIS PERSUASIVE LEADERTYPE: BALANCING THE PERSUASIVE WITH THE PRUDENT

For all his extraversion, Truman's personality was balanced by a strongly developed introverted quality, as well. Truman grew up with a "plain speaking" father who encouraged him to say what he meant, and mean what he said. This is reflected in his clear preference for Sensation (the auxiliary function of his personality type), and revealed in his strong Prudent LeaderType (Introverted Sensation). Evidence of this preference is his reading all 2,000 volumes in the local library—including the encyclopedias—and retaining a tremendous amount of historical trivia as an adult. He loved "to know the real facts." The most significant gift (according to him) he received as a child was *Great Men and Famous Women,* a collection of biographies—the details of which he memorized. He believed that men made history as opposed to the other way around, and that, "There is nothing new in the world except the history you do not know."

Early in life, his "steadfastness" impressed his teachers. One recalled "he would stand clear of his desk and square his shoulders before saying a word." His work on his father's farm (tracking some four hundred workers, seeing that they were paid every two weeks, and keeping the books) he described as "a very down-to-earth education," and flowed from his Prudent LeaderType. His first performance review as a bank clerk pointed out how he "watches everything closely and by his watchfulness, detects many errors which a careless boy would let slip through." This side of Truman's personality is revealed in various ways: from studying history in order to know the 'true facts' to reading biographies for application to his own life. This shows the balance in his personality was toward introverted Sensation. Sharing a strong Prudent LeaderType with George Washington (dominant in Washington; auxiliary in Truman), the parallels are interesting: he studied Cato (the Roman writer), and fashioned himself as Cincinnatus, just as Washington had; he also read modern scientific agriculture texts as had Washington in his day. Both had reading preferences for nonfiction, especially self-improvement.

The combination of this Extraverted Feeling and Introverted Sensation is revealed in a quote from one of his many letters to his lifelong sweetheart and wife, Bess Wallace: "You've no idea how experience teaches sympathy." In another he said, "I could die happy doing something for you."

In an effort to build a spiritual foundation, he joined the Masons, taking the spiritual teachings seriously, soon achieving Master Mason designation, enjoying both the comradeship and the rituals of the Masonic Lodge. This aspect of his personality speaks to his Extraverted Feeling: adopting a code of conduct or religion as one's own, doing what's proper in a social situation. When met on the street, and asked how he was doing, his standard reply was "I'm fine. How are you?" Not a fake platitude, but a genuine desire to maintain harmony in one's environment. He was all about collective expressions of civilization, whether it be going to church or going to the theater. In all cases, Harry strove to be self-effacing, respectful, and agreeable. His loyalty to others was born of his time in the Army, but reached its peak as part of the Pendergrast political machine (Tom Pendergrast was a political boss who controlled Kansas City and Jackson County, Missouri from 1925 to 1939, and launched Truman's career.). His loyalty to him was so widely known that Truman's enemies called him the "Senator from Pendergrast." Despite all his emphasis on relationships, however, he struggled with the press: "If they want to ask me some impudent questions, I'll try to give them some impudent answers." "Whenever the press quits abusing me, I'll know I'm in the wrong pew."

Even before becoming president, Truman clearly had an inclination for outward-directed action. He held many different jobs—some by choice (haberdasher), which didn't work out well, others he didn't choose (working on the family farm). He became respected as a leader as Captain, 129th Field Artillery in WWI. After returning a hero, he became a county judge, and then presiding judge in Jackson County, Missouri, before becoming a U.S. senator, and with one of the briefest terms as vice president in U.S. history (83 days). That Harry S Truman went from being a county judge in rural Missouri to the presidency in eleven years—and proved himself more than worthy of the task—is a testament to his character (active-positive) and type development.

CONTRASTS IN PERSONALITY WITH HIS PREDECESSOR

Even though extraverted like Roosevelt, Truman (ESFJ) represented a strong contrast to FDR (ENFP). As president, he completed the work his predecessor has begun in the realm of social welfare, seeking to expand FDR's New Deal into a Fair Deal (a nominal change reflective of differences in their personality types—from Innovating to Persuasive). Unfortunately, a coalition of southern Democrats and Republicans rejected the expansion. Truman's take on the change in their administrations reads like a textbook contrast of their personality types: "I want to keep my feet on the ground; I don't want any experiments; the American people have been through a lot of experiments and they want a rest from experiments." The Prudent, stable guardian within Truman was tired of FDR's non-stop Innovating.

His early interactions with Churchill were challenging, as the British prime minister had grown accustomed to the personality type of his predecessor, likely sharing many aspects with FDR. Roosevelt preferred to keep his options open, while Truman's preference was for reaching a conclusion and moving on to the next subject. At Potsdam (the Berlin suburb where he met Winston Churchill and Josef Stalin for the first time in a week-long conference which would shape post-war Europe), Truman complained, "I don't want to discuss, I want to decide." Churchill replied, "You want something in the bag each day," recognizing his Judging preference.

THE PERSUASIVE LEADERTYPE ON DISPLAY IN THE WHITE HOUSE

With no prior exposure to foreign affairs Truman's learning curve was very steep, given the seismic shifts in power among countries post-WWII. His strong preference for extraversion, I believe, led him to assert his leadership on the world stage, and not retreat into isolationism as the U.S. had following World War I. This position happened to align him with key Democrats — and Republicans — in Congress, making him the head of a powerful consensus, which sought a dominant role for the U.S. in foreign policy post-war. His extraversion is clearly seen in the energy he brought to the presidency. Befitting a chief executive envisioned by the authors of *The Federalist,* Truman energetically used the authority placed in the executive branch of government. He was known for cajoling a 'Do-Nothing' Congress. While not a particularly gifted speaker, he enjoyed meeting and greeting people; his handshake was "not (just) strong, but athletic." Throughout his presidency, Truman proved adept at turning plans and policies into reality by engaging those around him and spurring them into action.

Commenting on his decision-making process, Truman was fond of saying, "I never sit on a fence. I am either on one side or another. You know what I stand for." And he of course became famous for the sign on his Oval Office desk: *THE BUCK STOPS HERE.* Not one to vacillate, his decision-making was conclusive and final: "All my life, whenever it comes time to make a decision, I make it and forget about it." And rarely did Harry Truman change his mind. In many respects his personality was much like his father's: "A mighty good trader, John Truman," a neighbor recalled, "...very stubborn, but on the square." "Truman could be combative when his authority was challenged (General MacArthur's insubordination) and take decisive action when the responsibility was his (approving the use of the atomic bomb); but he did not seek out positions of leadership and was more comfortable with collegial relations than with domination." (Steven J. Rubenzer and Thomas R. Faschingbauer, *Personality, Character and Leadership in the White House*) It was after Potsdam that Truman was quoted as saying, "I like Joe Stalin." This is his Persuasive type going to lengths to look for rapport in relationships with an adversary.

The decision for which Truman is probably most remembered is the order to use an atomic weapon to end World War II—often perceived at odds with a Feeling preference which typically prefers diplomacy over war, negotiation over destruction. The following from his July 25, 1945 diary entry reveals his conscious rationale:

> "This weapon is to be used against Japan between now and August 10th. I have told the Sec. of War, Mr. Stimson, to use it so that military objectives and soldiers and sailors are the target and not women and children. ...we as the leader of the world for the common welfare cannot drop that terrible bomb on the old capital or the new. He and I are in accord. The target will be a purely military one and we will issue a warning statement asking the Japs to surrender and save lives."

Note his Feeling preference in the compassion for civilians, the 'one last try,' and the use of the phrase "in accord": It was important to Truman that he and Stimson were agreed on this. Many also have argued that Truman believed the atomic solution was the lesser of two evils: that a full-on ground assault to achieve Japanese surrender would have yielded much greater casualties — on both sides — than the two bombs. This argument would have appealed to Truman's Feeling side (i.e., saving lives, the "universal feeling" against war) and would have been given more weight as his Prudent side would have had no prior experience or established information on which to inform the decision. But, I believe it was his determination of which cities to bomb that is the more revealing of not only his Feeling preference, but also his whole type, and provides great insight into his unique challenge in executive decision-making.

Before Truman became president the decision to drop an atomic bomb was pretty much a *fait accompli*, hence not up for debate. The question on the table when he assumed office (April '45) was which cities to target. Military leaders favored Kyoto, Yokohama (just fifteen miles from the Imperial Palace in Tokyo) and Hiroshima — the first two intended to 'make a statement,' and 'cut off the head' of the Japanese empire by targeting its largest population centers. Stimson was against Kyoto being targeted, but the quote above hints at Truman's Feeling preference: that destroying both (or either) of those cities would be too destabilizing to Japanese culture: Kyoto was the former capital, and an intellectual and cultural center; Yokohama was a Tokyo suburb, and too close to the political heartbeat of the country. He obviously preferred industrial targets over civilian ones, but he apparently believed Hiroshima and Nagasaki (plus two other potential targets) were purely industrial, and failed to understand the nuance of the situation, or at least failed to probe further.

If you refer to Appendix 6, you'll see that two of Truman's weakest LeaderTypes were Visionary and Independent. Here are questions about deploying the atomic bomb that Thomas Jefferson and John Adams would have asked — and wanted answers to before deciding.

- What might I be assuming is similar in this situation, but in fact, is very different? That unlike German cities where workers lived in residential areas away from factories, Japanese workers typically lived very close to the military/industrial plants in which they worked. The notion that a target could be strictly military did not apply in this context.

- What different technique or technology is being used that I don't fully understand? A totally new weapon with an unprecedented level of destructive power and likely serious, long-term potential side-effects (i.e., many unknown unknowns) which severely limit its containment to strictly military targets.

- What might be some unintended consequences of using this technology? Russia may feel threatened, and accelerate development of its own capability, posing a greater future threat.

- What are the long-term strategic ramifications? That if we could develop this technology what's to keep other nations from developing it, potentially destabilizing the world?

- On what sound, reasoned, logical arguments am I making the case for this decision?

(Author's note: I realize these are all questions that seventy-plus years of hindsight now answer. My point is that these are not questions that would have occurred to Truman, given his personality type. And if not him, was there anyone on his team with those LeaderTypes to pose them? And if so, did that person have a voice? Chief executives must realize their strengths – and their limitations – in making highly impactful decisions, and intentionally seek opposing counsel.)

SUMMARY OF TRUMAN'S LEADERTYPE DEVELOPMENT

With preferences for Extraversion, Sensation, Feeling and Judging (ESFJ), Harry Truman's personality type likely developed in the following order (from most prevalent in his personality to least).

- **Persuasive** – his strong, interactive people-orientation; 'reading' and pleasing people; doing what was expected according to his faith, family, community, party and country. "Young Harry Truman saw the world as a place where fundamental values were given, not debated, and where individual characters shaped events." (James David Barber)

- **Proactive** – his busyness at an early age; his work on the farm—even if not by choice—involving multiple daily tasks.

- **Prudent** – his detailed knowledge of history; his penchant for memorization; his ability to master infinite details in complex situations; his willingness to listen carefully to others more knowledgeable.

- **Inclusive** – his authentic character, which comes into focus when he leads men into battle, and resulted in his ultimate success: "My whole political career is based on my war service and war associates." (Alfred Steinberg, *The Man from Missouri*) Upon returning from the war 'whole' he finally married his sweetheart of many years, Bess, at age 35. Unfortunately, this period also coincided with his failure in business.

About his midlife crisis, Jonathan Daniels wrote Truman "never really seemed to know what he wanted to do until he was nearly 40 years old." The idea that he was a 'failure' (like his father) was conquered when he returned home as a war hero, and made his move into politics (an interest he shared with his father). In the Pendergrast political machine Truman found a home where camaraderie, patronage and loyalty were valued — and all qualities, which played to his LeaderType strengths. He was so loyal that Richard Nixon remarked about him: "A lot of people admired the old bastard (Truman) for standing by people who were guilty as hell."

- **Take Charge** – his becoming comfortable with power, and taking charge of a body of men in a forceful way; his mediating of disputes and pronouncing rulings as a judge.

- **Innovating** – his mercurial move up in the world of politics, making new connections, and attaching his star to the New Deal government experiment in his ten years as U.S. senator.

- **Visionary** – his vision for the world, the significance of world events by the time he ascended to the presidency—especially his 1948 State of the Union message. "The cries from the reactionary quarters only prove that some people are afraid to look ahead."

- **Independent** – his post-presidential writings, characterized by the *NY Times* as 'pulling no punches.' Ironic that he came home (psychologically and literally) to Independence.

Harry Truman's popularity had reached a low point by the time he left office, and must have been very hard for a Persuasive leader who craved the trust and admiration of his people. In the years since, his reputation has recovered. Perhaps people collectively realized they'd been a little hard on the plainspoken man from Missouri, and that while he wasn't his charismatic predecessor, he did OK—even better than OK. Truman handled the difficult challenges he did using every aspect of his personality. He engaged the commitment of his country, served the needs of its people in conscientious style, and proved to be a leader that followers could trust.

Harry Truman – Summary Profile

Leadership positions: captain, Missouri National Guard, 129th Field Artillery (1917 – 1919); county judge for Eastern District, Jackson County, Missouri; presiding judge, Jackson County Court; U.S. senator; vice-president; president (1945 – 1953)

Age while president: 60 – 68

LeaderTypes:

Strongest: Persuasive
Supporting: Proactive, Prudent
Emerging: Take Charge (while president)
Weakest: Visionary, Independent

MBTI preferences (clarity):

- **Extraversion** (clear)
- **Sensation** (clear)
- **Feeling** (slight)
- **Judging** (clear)

Prominent Qualities:	Direct, Self-disciplined, Conscientious, Strong Character
Prominent Deficits:	Not Charismatic, Self-righteous (Columnist Samuel Grafton said while Truman was "vastly concerned with being right; he does not seem sufficiently concerned with getting the right things done.")
Motivational need(s):	Affiliation, Achievement
SCARF trigger(s):	Relatedness, Fairness, Certainty

COACHING THE PERSUASIVE LEADERTYPE IN YOU

If Persuasive is <u>not</u> your dominant LeaderType, reflect on these questions to strengthen Persuasive traits. These would come naturally to a Persuasive leader.

- What do other people need? What matters most to them? How are they involved / impacted?

- How do you seek and secure others' commitment? How do you influence or persuade them?

- How can you help others get what they need, as well as get what you need accomplished?

- How much do you trust your leader, your followers, or your peers? How can you build trust?

- To what extent do you feel trusted, respected, and liked by your leader, followers, and peers?

- To what extent does a lack of mutual trust impact your ability to accomplish your objectives?

If Persuasive is your dominant LeaderType, reflect on these questions to challenge you further.

- How do you customize your approach and interaction with people? How to get even better?

- What circumstances cause you to over use your Persuasive style? How might you mitigate this?

- How has your desire for harmony or diplomacy impacted your ability to be direct or candid?

- How might over protecting your team be creating dependency or reducing their resilience?

- How do you avoid over pleasing others? When do you insist people conform to your ways?

- When and how do you stand for your personal values, and not conform to corporate norms?

QUOTES FOR A PERSUASIVE JOURNEY

A companion's words of persuasion are effective. HOMER

I suppose leadership at one time meant muscles; but today it means getting along with people. INDIRA GANDHI

Management is nothing more than motivating people.
LEE IACOCCA

It all begins and ends with a customer-focused purpose that employees embrace and get passionate about. BILL GEORGE

What is important to another person must be as important to you as the other person is to you. STEPHEN COVEY

At the end of the day you bet on people not strategies.
LARRY BOSSIDY

People whose lives are affected by a decision must be part of the process of arriving at that decision. JOHN NAISBITT

Passion in any area of life is our soul's proclamation of being alive. Should passion fade, drama is always ready to take its place. PATRICK MCBRIDE

Life's most urgent question is, what are you doing for others?
MARTIN LUTHER KING, JR.

Section IV
The Fourth Element of Leadership: Drive Performance

Have a good plan, execute it violently, and do it today.
DAME MARJORIE SCARDINO

THE FINAL STAGE IN the process of leading is to Drive Performance - the culmination of the journey that began with grasping reality, envisioning success, and engaging commitment. Getting results through people requires a leader who can set clear goals and expectations, delegate tasks, equip members, remove roadblocks, inspect what they expect, give feedback, and hold herself and others accountable. Leaders must clarify not only the desired outcome, but also the desired means: clear rules of engagement for smart decision-making along the way. Only then can followers be empowered and held accountable for results. Upon successful completion, leaders should heed the words of retired professional soccer player, Mia Hamm: *Celebrate what you've accomplished, but raise the bar a little higher each time you succeed.*

What follows are two templates for driving performance, one extraverted (Theodore Roosevelt), and the other introverted (John Adams). In a Take Charge and

Independent way, these leaders show us how to Drive Performance, the fourth Element of Leadership.

Chapter Nine:
The Take Charge LeaderType Theodore Roosevelt, 26th President of the United States

THE TAKE CHARGE BRAND: MAKE-IT-HAPPEN DRIVER

THINK OF TEDDY ROOSEVELT leading the Rough Riders up San Juan Hill in Cuba, and you get the image of the Take Charge leader. He drives through life, surrounded by a firestorm, always intent on making things happen and getting things done—whatever the cost. He will never, ever be accused of inaction.

Throughout his presidency—and his life—Roosevelt applied a 'take-no-prisoners' approach to every situation. Whether leading a charge on the battlefront, or exposing corruption in the police force, or battling captains of industry in crusading for fairness, he mustered the internal and external resources he needed to forge ahead and win the day. He is known for his incredible tenacity, and ability to remain focused on the end goal, even in times of tumult.

Having good principles for dealing with the realities we encounter is the most important driver of how well we handle them. RAY DALIO

HOW THE TAKE CHARGE LEADERTYPE FUNCTIONS

A Take Charge LeaderType focuses on what needs to be done, now and how. He secures resources and strategizes the way forward. He organizes, sequences, and deploys the means to achieve the team's goal. He identifies, prioritizes, and delegates tasks and responsibilities to most efficiently reach measurably defined targets. Then he leads the team into whatever challenges arises, never giving up, until they've hit their mark.

The Take Charge LeaderType establishes and abides by principles and rules of engagement, always keeping the end goal in mind. It is all about using whatever means (within one's ethical principles) to drive through any obstacles, and ultimately accomplish your objective.

The Take Charge LeaderType works well within the system to achieve established goals—until he encounters that bureaucratic morass, inefficient process, incompetent resource, or lazy, unmotivated individual. He will move directly into and through that barrier, using whatever resources necessary—including the people on his team—to forge ahead to the end-goal.

Strategy gets you on the playing field, but execution pays the bills. GORDON EUBANKS

TAKE CHARGE LEADERTYPE STRENGTHS

- Clarifying roles, goals; sequencing, delegating tasks to efficiently achieve a desired end
- Setting 'stretch' targets to exceed expectations; enabling execution by removing obstacles
- Reaching objectives through securing, allocating and organizing resources to get results
- Planning and prioritizing tasks; coordinating to implement plans in the most efficient way
- Structuring/organizing surroundings for optimal effectiveness; setting templates, policies
- Setting performance standards and criteria; making tough organizational/staff decisions
- Holding self, others accountable; never accepting excuses when it comes to making evaluations

No decision has been made unless carrying it out in specific steps has become someone's work assignment and responsibility. PETER F. DRUCKER

TAKE CHARGE LEADERTYPE STRUGGLES

- Dealing with incompetence, errors, delays, lack of accountability or aggressive criticism
- Dealing with barriers to executing efficiently, or lack of urgency on the part of others
- Reaching conclusions or making decisions too quickly, often with insufficient data
- Neglecting or dismissing others' values, concerns, needs, or feelings in a situation

- Listening; being perceived as condescending, domineering, overconfident or arrogant
- Building consensus through dialogue; impatience with unstructured, group processes

The best executive is the one who has sense enough to pick good men to do what he wants done, and self-restraint enough to keep from meddling with them while they do it. THEODORE ROOSEVELT

A TAKE CHARGE LEADERTYPE IN THE WHITE HOUSE

Read on and see why Teddy Roosevelt is the personification of the Take Charge LeaderType.

THEODORE ROOSEVELT: THE TAKE-CHARGE PRESIDENT

TAKING CHARGE OF THE PRESIDENCY AND THE NATION

In Theodore Roosevelt's presidency we see the unambiguous results of a Take Charge leader.

- Extending broad executive power: From the Civil War until the late 1800s, the balance of power was with Congress; with Roosevelt, a shift already in the making gained momentum, and the balance of power swung clearly toward the executive branch.

- Expanding nationalism to international arenas (e.g., "I took Panama."): Beyond creating a new country out of another (Colombia), Roosevelt sought to rid the Americas of the formerly colonizing Europeans. (The irony of creating a 'colony' in the form of the Panama Canal Zone was apparently lost on him.) He also wanted to annex Hawaii, intervene in Cuba, and sail the U.S. navy around the world in a show of force. His tenure presaged America's leadership of the free world — a direct consequence, I believe, of his Take Charge style.

- Taking on big business and driving reforms through Congress: Roosevelt used the power of his office to combat capitalists and unions alike; he insisted on a Square Deal for every man. He saw himself as a champion of right over wrong and positioned himself as referee in numerous power struggles — even winning a Nobel Peace Prize for mediating an end to the Russo-Japanese War.

- Establishing protection and conservation for America's natural resources and environment: By taking charge of the agenda, and playing grand arbitrator, Roosevelt balanced the laissez-faire lumber and mining interests with John Muir's Preservationists to promote his Conservationist ideals. The result: the most lasting impact any president has had on the physical landscape of the United States, by creating the U.S. Forest Service, five national parks, eighteen new national monuments, fifty-one bird preserves, four game reserves, and 150 national forests.

Theodore Roosevelt asserted himself on every person, institution, and landscape he encountered. Whether it was setting his sights on his bride-to-be Alice ("She won't have me, but I'm going to have *her!*"), climbing the Matterhorn while on his honeymoon, carving out an existence as a rancher in the Badlands of South Dakota, or taking charge of the Board of Police Commissioners of New York City and fighting graft and corruption, or even winning over the press, (to borrow Ryan Holiday's book title) the obstacle WAS the way. He loved a good fight, but he loved to win more. This was a man who shook his fist at J.P. Morgan and took on the powerbrokers of his party in his zeal for justice and reform and his fight for common principles, saying "There can be no compromise in the enforcement of the law," earning him the nickname, Trust-Buster.

Even TR's choice to go into politics (an unsuitable profession for someone of his class) was a means to an end: he wanted to leave not just any mark, but a big mark, and the way he saw to do that was power, to be in charge. (Of McClelland's motivation theory, he seems equally balanced between the need for Power and the need for Achievement.) And although Washington and Jackson possessed this LeaderType as an auxiliary to their dominant LeaderTypes, Roosevelt's (as dominant) is the best example of a Take Charge leader among U.S. presidents.

Jung said, "This type of man elevates the objective reality, or an objectively oriented intellectual formula, into the ruling principle, not only for himself, but for his whole environment...By this formula, good and evil are measured...Everything that agrees with the formula is right, everything that contradicts is wrong...If the formula is broad enough, this type may play a...reformer or public prosecutor..." For Theodore Roosevelt, that formula is summarized in this quote: "Justice consists not in being neutral between right and wrong, but in finding out the right and upholding it, wherever found, against the wrong." Jung said that very often for this type, "the end justifies the means."

Roosevelt's preference—and strength—in influencing others (whether writing or debating) was clearly 'push,' not 'pull.' He would pound away at his point when speaking—and literally pound one fist into the palm of his other hand—to correct someone's error or misconception, or to emphatically make his case. On the receiving end, however, it felt more like bullying, arrogance, or imperialism. A *World* reporter observed, "When he asks a question, Mr. Roosevelt shoots it at the poor trembling policeman, as he would shoot a bullet at a coyote...he shows a set of teeth calculated to unnerve the bravest of the Finest." Nathan Miller, in *Theodore Roosevelt: A Life,* said, "Roosevelt wasted no time in grabbing the Police Department by the scruff of its neck and giving it a good shaking up. Good men (however) were given generous praise and promotions." Perhaps not to the degree that his younger cousin, Franklin, demonstrated it, but Theodore knew he needed strategic alliances to achieve his ends. He cultivated loyalty, however, to a cause—not to his person. He recognized his power was never absolute—nor should it be—and that it must always be in service to a nobler vision.

When he took over the Civil Service Commission, he remarked "You can guarantee that I intend to hew the line, and let the chips fall where they will." When he was attacked, he attacked right back — blow for blow. He summed up his pride in what he did to Senator Henry Cabot Lodge: "We stirred up things well." He liked a good fight; in fact, he boxed from an early age into the presidency (the reason for his blindness in one eye). One of his favorite expressions when faced with challenging weather conditions or difficult situations was, "Isn't this *bully?*" It was almost as if the contest — whether the force of winds, or a fight in the ring — gave him energy to rebuff and conquer the opposition. He originated the label 'bully pulpit' for the White House and used his position, his platform, and his relationship with the press to leverage his influence. "He was a walking day of judgment," said the naturalist, John Burroughs. Woodrow Wilson, his political adversary in the 1912 election, called him "the most dangerous man of the age."

Roosevelt preaching "Walk softly, and carry a big stick" (a West African proverb) was, in his practicing of it, only half-right: he spoke loudly, and loved to not only carry a stick, but brandish it often. The 'big stick' formula translated into beliefs about the United States — that the key to its greatness lies in its ability to put aside petty differences in submission to the 'great nation' cause.

His extraversion is without question: "Get action. Seize the moment. Man was never intended to become an oyster." He literally wrote the book, *A Strenuous Life* and practiced what it preached: he once played ninety games of tennis in one day! He was so focused on externals such as the environment, animals, birds (he wanted to be another Audubon) that he would become absorbed to the point he would ignore his own needs. Once, while reading in front of a fire it was only the smell of his shoes burning that diverted his attention away from the book he was reading. On that point, he was a voracious reader (sometimes reading one or two books a night, and could reportedly quote entire paragraphs five years later), and a prodigious author (of more than thirty-five books). While outwardly gregarious and assertive, he was capable of tremendous focus and reflection. Most people believed, said newspaperman Lincoln Steffens that, "he never thinks, that every act is born of the impulse of the moment." They were wrong, he said, "He thinks before he acts." To which I would add, very quickly. Never content to walk, he was always in a hurry or in a race he intended to win. Because of his very clear preference for extraversion, he had not only developed Extraverted Thinking, but also Extraverted Intuition and Sensation. "No other president ever enjoyed the Presidency as I did! No President has ever enjoyed himself as much as I." A British diplomat and friend of the Roosevelts said of him: "You must always remember the President is about 6 [years old]." Teedie (his nickname) definitely claimed his 'eternal child.'

Typical of extraverts, his greatest regrets stemmed from not acting (for example, not running for mayor of New York), and speaking too soon when asked if he would seek the Oval Office a second time at the end of his seven-plus years in office. About running for mayor, he said, "the prize was very great; the expense would have been trivial and the chances of success very good." Numerous quotes reveal he associated action with light and inaction with darkness: to try and fail was far superior to not even trying. In times of grief and sorrow, he introverted—and then got busy to counter its effects: "Black care rarely sits behind the rider whose pace is fast enough," he said. Still, TR would not let his hopes and dreams ("I must be wanting to be President—every young man does!") override his focus on doing the best job he could in whatever his current role. This shows the relationship between his auxiliary Visionary LeaderType and his Take Charge LeaderType: "There is no use in looking ahead (Intuition)," he wrote as governor, "as regards one's personal interests, though there is every use in shaping one's career so as to conduct it along firmly grounded principles and policies." (Extraverted Thinking)

HOW ROOSEVELT'S TAKE CHARGE LEADERTYPE WAS FORMED

His early life was a struggle to overcome asthma, allergies and extreme near-sightedness, to build his physique and strength ("I'll make my body!"), and to live up to the dreams of his father ("the only man of whom I was ever really afraid"). Some attribute his aggressiveness to overcompensation for his physical inferiority. His biographer, Nathan Miller remarked that Teedie's "metamorphosis from sickly, scrawny boy into masterful man became a lifelong model and standard of measuring men, social groups, and nations." This reveals how Take Charge leaders look for external standards and benchmarks by which to judge—themselves and others.

Calling himself "nervous and timid," as a child he loved adventure stories and was himself a great storyteller at an early age. "I had a great admiration for men who were fearless and who could hold their own in the world, and I had a great desire to be like them." "Afraid? Of course, I'm afraid. But what you've to do is look and act as though you weren't. Then by and by you won't be." He was very evaluative of himself — even at an early age, taking inventory of his strengths and weaknesses at age 10: "Health: good. Lessons: good. Play hours: bad. Appetite: good. Clothes: greasy. Shoes: holey. Hair: more 'a-la-Mop' than ever. Nails: dirty." Later on, in describing a close friend, "As athletes we are about equal; he rows best; I run best; he can beat me sailing or swimming; I can beat him wrestling or boxing; I am best with the rifle, he with the shotgun, etc. etc." He also used his father as the example against which he judged other men: particularly their profanity, drinking, and personal ethics, but also their virility and competitiveness. His father's admonishment to him upon leaving for Harvard (one of the last times he'd see him as he died suddenly of stomach cancer when TR was 19): "Take care of your morals first, your health next and finally your studies." True to his type, Roosevelt, took these prioritized directives seriously, and implemented a regimen at Harvard to execute them efficiently. Summing up the Roosevelt family (and Theodore, particularly) from a once-outsider's point of view, his mother said, "They think they are just, but they are hard in a way."

Before befriending, he checked people out very carefully, researching their background and determining their suitableness for acquaintanceship. One arena in which he acknowledged falling short of his father's footsteps was the elder Roosevelt's devotion to, and works in support of, charitable institutions. "I tried faithfully to do what Father had done but I did it poorly," he told a friend. "In the end, I found out that we each have to work in his own way to our best." (The other way in which he differed with his father was in the elder's refusal to fight with the Union Army during the Civil War, choosing instead to do relief work. 'Thee,' as his father was called, was a humanitarian and philanthropist.) Despite his patrician upbringing, and being told politicians were 'rough and brutal and unpleasant to deal with,' he chose politics. Few leaders have ever wielded power as comfortably and effectively as TR. At age 23, by his own admission, Theodore Roosevelt was a political hack. Widely known for being a populist crusader, he wrote in 1903: "My business is to see fair play, among all men, capitalists and wage workers" and to tackle domestic and foreign crises "with immediate and vigorous executive action." This was his Take Charge LeaderType, in unambiguous terms, taking on the world.

As assistant secretary of the Navy, he said, "The Secretary is away, and I am having immense fun running the navy." He took advantage of the secretary's summer vacation, and presented then-President McKinley with a strategic war plan to oust Spain from Cuba. That plan was, to a large extent, followed when war broke out a year later. Many leaders conveniently forget what they did in their ascent to power. It is well accepted that Roosevelt was one of the most honest about his faults, failures, and weaknesses as he was about his accomplishments. However, in his *Autobiography,* rather than talk about the less-than-successful outcomes, he said volumes by what he didn't discuss.

BEYOND HIS TAKE CHARGE LEADERTYPE

Whenever TR was faced with negative emotions or challenging relationships he went within, often pursuing a solitary activity like rowing, swimming, riding or simply reflecting. His Feeling function flowed unconsciously inward...like being in love with himself. Upon seeing the Egyptian ruins, TR recorded in his diary "On seeing this stately remain of former glory, I *felt* a great deal but I *said* nothing...it gave rise to thoughts of the ineffable, the unutterable; thoughts which you cannot express, which cannot be uttered, which cannot be answered until after The Great Sleep." Jung said this function of his personality operates in a way "completely oblivious to the individual...a secret self-seeking which gives a selfish twist to actions that are in themselves disinterested." He was not only comfortable in the spotlight, he relished it. His nephew quipped, "He wanted to be the bride at every wedding, and the corpse at every funeral." This reveals his triggering by Status. That he fully engaged in every event he attended shows his considerable extraversion. If he didn't originate the idiom, he certainly epitomized it: Theodore Roosevelt was the life of the party.

Theodore's Extraverted Thinking was served by Intuition in the auxiliary position: As a child he often played make-believe games and continued to have an active and vivid imagination into adulthood. He was creative, artistic, inventive, and quick to grasp new ideas and trends: H.G. Wells called him "a very symbol of the creative will in man." His principles and reforms were informed by his view of where things would lead if unchanged or uncorrected. He believed that America was headed for a class war...that unbridled greed of financiers and businessmen juxtaposed with the intolerable living conditions of workers would lead to a much worse crisis if not averted. That he believed he should (and could) adjust/correct the balance of capital and labor, and took steps to do so, demonstrates his Take Charge supported by Visionary and Innovating. Finally, avoiding the opposite of Innovating (Prudent), "[Theodore Roosevelt] seldom allowed himself to become immersed in details. He simply sampled," noted Edwin C. Hargrove.

In the final analysis, TR was a thought leader long before thought leadership became popular. His definition, though, differs from what most would think: "I did not divine how the people were going to think; I simply made up my mind what they ought to think." This reflects not only asserting his views on the world, but also that he was not going to be swayed by public opinion polls—something which he detested in Woodrow Wilson. One cannot ignore TR's tremendous intellect—and capacity for intelligent conversation around diverse subjects in conjunction with his thought leadership. "In one afternoon," said his son Archie, "I have heard him speak to the foremost Bible student of the world, a prominent ornithologist, a French diplomat and general, all of whom agreed that Father knew more about the subjects on which they had specialized than they did."

TR'S TYPE DEVELOPMENT OVER HIS LIFETIME

Roosevelt's personality preferences for Extraversion, Intuition, Thinking, Judging yield a unique arc to his development.

- **Take Charge** –exhibiting control; "I will make my body (be stronger)," conquering asthma; "I took Panama." This quote sums up his Take Charge philosophy: "If we stand idly by, if we seek merely swollen, slothful ease and ignoble peace, if we shrink from the hard contests where men must win at hazard of their lives and at the risk of all they hold dear, then the bolder and stronger peoples will pass us by, and will win for themselves the domination of the world."

- **Innovating** – continuous, voracious learning; active imagination; seeking the new/different

- **Visionary** – establishing his life's ambition to be president, interpreting others' motives

- **Independent** – researching the latest ideas; Michael Beschloss wrote of his time in the state legislature, "He was something of a maverick whom his party leaders could not manage."

His greatest personal crisis happened at age 27, when his wife and his mother died on the same Valentine's Day. I believe his going to Badlands was to deal with his 'shadow': to introvert his feelings about what had happened, and to solidify his authenticity. After midlife, these LeaderTypes came into greater use.

- **Persuasive** – in office, becoming more collaborative, striking compromises, negotiating or mediating; influencing people to his point of view; insisting on loyalty, and attacking when they were not. After leaving office, he mercilessly criticized Taft (his successor) to the point of causing Taft to cry and bewilderingly remark, "He was my closest friend."

- **Proactive** – safari hunting; going down the River of Doubt, and almost dying ("I had to go; it was my last chance to be a boy.")

- **Prudent** – writing historical biographies throughout his life (e.g., *The Winning of the West*); memorizing: being able to recite chapters of books several years after reading.

- **Inclusive** – dying before this LeaderType could be fully realized, and the lack of it showed. In an essay in *Presidential Leadership*, John McCain said of him, "He abhorred multiculturalists' adulation of diversity as more important than national unity and patriotism." Roosevelt decried the "over-exaltation of the little community at the expense of the great nation," paving the way for strong nationalism, which I believe is the political hallmark of a Take Charge leader.

Theodore Roosevelt's personality shaped not only his leadership and his Presidency; it shaped THE Presidency and the country in the nascent 20th century.

- He was drawn to a challenge and vowed to conquer it: "Far better it is to dare mighty things, to win glorious triumphs, even though checkered by failure, than to rank with those poor spirits who neither enjoy much nor suffer much, because they live in that grey twilight that knows neither victory nor defeat." Seeing the world as his challenge, Roosevelt would set in motion the United States becoming a global power.

- His preference was clearly for Extraversion; his bias was for action and initiative: "The only man who makes no mistakes is the man who never does anything." He set a robust example of an activist president. For the rest of the century, presidents would swing from introverted isolationism to extraverted expansionism, in reaction to his model: either wanting to be seen as like him, or distancing themselves from him, as Wilson did. I think part of his great disappointment with Taft, his successor, was that Taft was not more like him, or perhaps didn't put up a strong enough fight: Taft was almost his exact opposite personality type. Their personality results on one particular facet of the NEO-PI highlight this. Of all U.S. Presidents, TR's Assertiveness score was the highest (100th percentile); Taft's score was the lowest. I find Take Charge leaders crave a good fight. They want a matchup with a worthy opponent for a couple of reasons. A strong competitor challenges them to be stronger (i.e., they get better), and winning against a weaker rival isn't much fun—nor does it yield much glory.

- He showed considerable balance in his personality in these quotes: "Keep your eyes on the stars, and your feet on the ground." (The balancing of Intuition and Sensation); and "Nobody cares how much you know, until they know how much you care." (The balancing of Thinking and Feeling).

- He had a strong sense of Fairness: "A man who is good enough to shed his blood for his country is good enough to be given a square deal afterwards. More than that no man is entitled to, and less than that no man shall have."

TR brought to bear every resource at his disposal in taking on every challenge faced. He wielded power comfortably. He asserted himself unabashedly. He boxed his way through life, but in the end, it was the punch he didn't see coming that knocked him out. Of his passing, Thomas R. Marshall, vice president under Wilson, said: "Death had to take him in his sleep, for if he was awake there'd have been a fight." Theodore Roosevelt took charge of himself, the nation, and the hemisphere, and in so doing, set the mold for many an industrial and political leader in the 20th century. If he'd chosen an epitaph for his tombstone, my guess is that it would have been his favorite expression, summing up his life experience: "That was BULLY!"

Theodore Roosevelt – Summary Profile

Leadership positions: assemblyman New York State; commissioner U.S. Civil Service; police commissioner New York City; assistant secretary of the navy; lt. colonel; colonel, 1st U.S. volunteer Cavalry Regiment (Rough Riders); governor of New York; U.S. vice-president; U.S. president (1901 – 1909)

Age while president: 42 – 50

LeaderTypes:

Strongest: Take Charge
Supporting: Innovating, Proactive, Visionary
Emerging: Persuasive (while president)
Weakest: Inclusive

MBTI preferences (clarity):

- **Extraversion** (very clear)
- **Intuition** (clear)
- **Thinking** (slight)
- **Judging** (clear)

Prominent Qualities:	Positive Emotions, Assertive, Ambitious
Prominent Deficits:	Not modest
Motivational need(s):	Achievement, Power
SCARF trigger(s):	Status, Fairness, Autonomy

COACHING THE TAKE CHARGE LEADERTYPE IN YOU

If Take Charge is <u>not</u> your dominant LeaderType, consider these questions to develop it.

- Given your mission, what goals and expectations will drive your team to reach its vision?

- What principles guide you/your team? What factors/ focus areas are critical to your success?

- What evidence supports your case? What consequences logically flow from your decision?

- How will you structure your group's work for maximum efficiency? How will you streamline it?

- How will you clarify roles, responsibilities, and interdependencies for effective operation?

- What is the most efficient sequencing of tasks/actions to reach your target by the deadline?

- What benchmarks, performance standards, or metrics will you put in place to ensure success?

If Take Charge is your dominant LeaderType, consider these questions to challenge you:

- In what situations does this style work for you? How do you know? When does it not work?

- What feedback has been toughest for you to hear and act on? What caused you to accept it?

- What is most important to you personally? How satisfied are you with how you exhibit that?

- When do you need to listen to your conscience? What would be three consequences of that?

- How much do you respect your team? Do they know it? How can you be more inclusive?

- What impact would fully valuing each team member have on productivity and performance?

- What good can you do without letting anyone know you did it? When will you act on that?

QUOTES FOR A TAKE CHARGE JOURNEY

What you cannot enforce, do not command. SOPHOCLES

His mental processes are plain—one knows what he will do, And can logically predicate his finish by his start.
RUDYARD KIPLING

Setting a goal is not the main thing. It is deciding how you will go about achieving it and staying with that plan. TOM LANDRY

Strategy is easy, implementation is hard...
RAYMOND W. SMITH

What you measure is what you get. ROBERT S. KAPLAN AND DAVID P. NORTON

Effective leaders check their performance. They write down, "What do I hope to achieve if I take on this assignment?" ... and then come back and check their performance against goals. This way, they find out whether they picked the truly important things to do. PETER DRUCKER

Chapter Ten:
The Independent LeaderType John Adams, 2ⁿᵈ President of the United States

THE INDEPENDENT BRAND: RESOLUTE THOUGHT LEADER

THE INDEPENDENT LEADERTYPE IN you is that which will ensure that whatever plan, structure, or strategy you put in place has been rigorously tested and passed logical inspection. She will challenge and debate ideas until proven sound. She will clarify her thoughts after careful consideration from multiple perspectives. She will apply thorough analysis to any problem or situation before taking any action. Using her well-ordered mind, she always seeks a deep understanding of any given issue.

John Adams is a stirring example of the Independent LeaderType. Often portrayed as the great intellectual in the cadre of our founding fathers, he applied thoughtful analysis to the monumental problems facing the fledgling nation. He sifted through volumes of law, logic, and philosophy, using them as raw materials to build his case for a perfectly structured government. We can see in the language of the Declaration of Independence and U.S. Constitution the results of Adams' thoughtful analyses. He was the preeminent thought leader of the American Revolution.

Thinking is the hardest work there is, which is probably the reason why so few people engage in it.
HENRY FORD

HOW THE INDEPENDENT LEADERTYPE FUNCTIONS

The Independent LeaderType seeks to freshly define every situation, building her own, brand-new model using established evidence. She always tries to understand and apply the correct framework, principles and assumptions to the current challenge or issue. Toward that end, she defines precise categories, and mentally organizes and classifies information using a logically tested framework.

The Independent LeaderType objectively questions and theorizes to clearly understand and explain how data fits her mental model. She then decides and/or reaches an internally consistent answer by applying detached, analytical reasoning.

The Independent LeaderType lends almost incalculable value to any organization facing seemingly insoluble problems. She will look at it from multiple perspectives, poking holes in any assumptions, until she arrives at a reliable answer. Her original analysis often uncovers solutions that hadn't occurred to anyone else.

Nothing has such power to broaden the mind as the ability to investigate systematically and truly all that comes under thy observation in life.
MARCUS AURELIUS

INDEPENDENT LEADERTYPE STRENGTHS

- Defining a situation, issue, or problem in-depth; making sound evidence-based decisions
- Analyzing root causes; weighing pros/cons; seeing logical consequences; finding flaws
- Setting and achieving high standards of excellence; pointing out performance gaps
- Providing impartial critique of work; explaining the rationale/parameters of the job to do
- Establishing categories for information, ideas; structuring thoughts on logic, principles
- Showing curiosity about why/how things work; leveraging inputs to maximize output

Liberty is a self-determining power in an intellectual agent. It implies thought and choice and power.
JOHN ADAMS

INDEPENDENT LEADERTYPE STRUGGLES

- Abiding by strict rules or regulations, or micromanagement; dealing with incompetence
- Operating when logic is questioned or absent, or when data does not fit model/framework

- Over-thinking issues; analysis-paralysis; seeking perfection/precision over 'good enough'
- Dealing with peoples' emotions, passions, or needs; being seen as too critical/impersonal
- Accepting popular opinion; reaching group consensus; seeing the value of collaboration
- Challenging others' thinking seen as interrogating; oblivious about insensitivity to others

THE INDEPENDENT LEADERTYPE IN THE WHITE HOUSE

Read the following profile of President John Adams to see how the Independent LeaderType functions in real life.

JOHN ADAMS: THE INDEPENDENT LEADER

HIS NATURE BECAME THE NATION'S PATH

John Adams was the intellect behind America's Revolution. Called "our colossus on the floor" (perhaps a double entendre) by Thomas Jefferson, another delegate described him as "the man to whom the country is most indebted for the great measure of independence." This "Atlas of Independence" gives us the clearest example of an Independent LeaderType at the top of his game. And his game was the law; more precisely, the process of law. As a thought leader, he literally put forward his "Thoughts on Government" (1776), counterpunching Thomas Paine's *Common Sense*. He didn't put much stock in human nature and abhorred the French Revolution for the chaos it created — all of which put him at odds with Thomas Jefferson's republicanism and adoration of the French experiment. But he held fast to his convictions no matter what the cost to his friendships. More than any other founding figure (including George Washington), his integrity was without question. In short, the lawyer from Braintree was the brain behind what became the United States of America.

He believed that leadership should do what was in the best interest of the people — which he believed he knew best. He did not put much faith in human nature or the basic goodness of man. He was sarcastic, cutting and condescending. He valued his autonomy and independence and did not take personal interest in others, nor wish to cultivate relationships with anyone other than his wife, Abigail. Adams enjoyed pondering abstract ideas and theories and was goal-oriented. He thought there was something wrong with someone who didn't know themselves and their life goals by the time they were 25.

THE INDEPENDENT LEADERTYPE IN CLEAR RELIEF IN NATIONAL POLITICS AND THE WHITE HOUSE

True to his Independent LeaderType, Adams was single-minded in his framing of the house of how America would govern. And he was clear in the knowledge that rebelling, overthrowing, and tearing down the structure of English rule would be the easy part. The much harder task, he knew, would be rebuilding it. But that is what enticed him — the challenge of creating an edifice that would stand for centuries. And regarding the design, he definitely had opinions. In a letter to Abigail he reveals the foundation of his case for representation over direct democracy: "Democracy has never been and never can be so durable as aristocracy or monarchy; but while it lasts, it is bloodier than either…Remember, democracy never lasts long. It soon wastes, exhausts, and murders itself. There never was a democracy yet that did not commit suicide." He basically didn't trust people—or rather the capacity of a group of people to govern itself without checks and balances. "Individuals have mastered themselves; nations and bodies of men, never." Realizing he might not win the ultimate debate on democracy, he architected three branches of government. Probably more to him than anyone else, America owes the way it is ruled today to John Adams' Independent thought leadership.

While Adams was clearly brilliant when it came to the theory of government, he was clueless when it came to running one. More specifically, he lacked skills of organization, as well as collaboration in the forging of policy, communication of that policy, and alignment needed to support policy. His inherent need for autonomy and his fiery temperament made it difficult for him to function in a team setting, much less lead a Cabinet. He was particularly subject to anger management issues; however, he did take counsel from his comparably strong-willed wife, Abigail Adams. She challenged his thinking, often sharing and reinforcing her husband's views.

The presidency has been called the least successful chapter of his life—but not according to him: "I had complete and perfect success, and left my country at peace with all the world, upon terms consistent with the honor and interest of the United States, and with all our relations with other nations, and all our obligations by the law of nations or treaties...and a treasury full of five millions (sic) of dollars. This was all done step by step, against perpetual oppositions, clamor and reproaches, such as no other President ever had to encounter (the irony that he was only the second president should not be lost here), and with a more feeble, divided, and incapable support than has ever fallen to the lot of any administration before or since." Still, he realized "Mausoleums, statues, monuments will never be erected to me." Benjamin Franklin famously remarked that Adams was "always an honest man, often a wise one, but sometimes and in some things absolutely out of his senses." There has been some speculation that his volatile temperament may have been physiological (hyperthyroidism), and that may have been so, but I believe it to be the result of his tendency toward fierce independence given his personality type.

In addition to being triggered by Autonomy, Adams was triggered by Status — especially around his intelligence and knowledge. Others of this type might be triggered around their competence (i.e., Who's the smartest person in the room?). For Adams, his Persuasive LeaderType was his Achilles heel. He resisted and disdained anything that smacked of popularity, mass appeal (such as Thomas Paine's *Common Sense*). Jung said leaders of this this type have a "horror of publicity"; in today's terms that would mean a distaste for hype, hyperbole, effusive sentiment, popularity, playing to opinion polls, and/or being politically correct. John Adams was a brilliant and blunt-spoken man of independent mind.

Thomas Jefferson summed him up this way to James Madison in 1787: "He is vain, irritable, and a bad calculator of the force and probable effect of the motives which govern men. This is the entire ill which can possibly be said of him. He is as disinterested as the Being who made him. He is profound in his views and accurate in his judgment, except where knowledge of the world is necessary to form a judgment." Adams was almost willful in his refusal to engage in the everyday art of political persuasion, once stating his intention to "quarrel with both parties and every individual in each before I would subjugate my understanding, or prostitute my tongue or pen to either." As yet another example of his Extraverted Feeling being inferior and least developed, he detested political parties because they were about reaching group consensus via compromise on policies.

The Adams presidency was fraught with errors of his own making. The most effective of the early presidents had goals they privately made known, even though they did not advance formal programs. Adams, however, appears to have taken office with no larger goal than the virtuous conduct of his duties. Shortly after he assumed office in 1797, hostilities erupted with France. While seeking a diplomatic settlement Adams engaged in confrontational rhetoric and posturing, only to send an emissary to France to seek peace. Then, in the midst of swirling controversy, he retreated to Massachusetts for seven months. Disappearing for months at a time turned into a pattern in his presidency, again reflecting his independent spirit. Another reflection of his lack of many Persuasive tendencies is his disregard for how important a loyal Cabinet was. He looked at the holders

of those offices in an almost totally abstract and imper-
sonal way: having earned their role and responsibility by
virtue of their service to country and their competence—
not their loyalty to him. He also saw no need to 'team
build,' and spent much time in Massachusetts—or trav-
eling back and forth. And while he was away members
of his Cabinet took matters into their own hands. Intense
partisan rivalry was not something Adams was well
equipped to handle given his personality. Oblivious to
any need for influence or persuasion, he probably won-
dered why others couldn't see the logic of what needed
to be done. It was abundantly clear to him.

Insistent on being consistent with his own principles of
strategic independence, Adams stayed out of the 'quasi
war' with France. He was a strict noninterventionist: "I
have well fixed it in my Mind as a Principle, that every
Nation has a Right to that Religion and Government,
which it chooses, and as long as any People please themselves in these great Points, I am determined they shall
not displease me." Another principle he, like Jefferson,
held dear was that if democracy had any hope it rested
on an educated public: "Laws for the liberal education
of youth, especially of the lower class of people, are so
extremely wise and useful, that, to a humane and generous mind, no expense for this purpose would be thought
extravagant." He further believed that children should
be instructed in the cost of freedom, and what democracy
required if it were to survive.

A DEEPER LOOK AT THE INTROVERTED THINKING TYPE

In personality type and beyond there were definite contrasts between Adams (MBTI: INTP) and his predecessor, Washington (MBTI: ISTJ). Physically, Washington was tall, thin, erect and soft-spoken. Adams was short, rotund, unimposing and susceptible to rages. Adams has been variously described as irritable, self-righteous, suspicious, and contentious. Washington and Jefferson were attentive to the need to structure their administrations, whereas the Adams presidency was an organizational disaster. Adams retained Washington's Cabinet with seeming obliviousness to the potential disloyalty of its members — one of whom was allied with his greatest rival, Alexander Hamilton. This is yet another example of how Adams downplayed the importance of trusting relationships and was ignorant to internecine strife. Not at all the 'polite-to-all' Washington, Adams was not one to mince words, calling things (and people) like he saw them:

- About Thomas Paine's *Common Sense*: "A poor, ignorant, malicious, shortsighted, crapulous mass."

- About Alexander Hamilton: "The bastard brat of a Scotch peddler."

- On the vice presidency (to which he was elected twice, serving under GW): "The most insignificant office of government that ever the Invention of man ever contrived or his Imagination conceived."

- On why Thomas Jefferson should write the *Declaration*, and not him: "I am obnoxious, suspected, and unpopular. You are very much otherwise [and] you can write ten times better than I can." This reveals a couple of things about an Independent LeaderType: 1) impartial self-critique; 2) recognition of superior talent when confronted with it. Where Adams diverges from healthier versions of this type is that he was very jealous of Jefferson's ability and the worship he would ultimately receive for writing the *Declaration*.

Jung describes this type at its conscious, fully functioning, cognitive best: "The thinking of the introverted type is positive and synthetic in developing ideas which approximate more and more to the eternal validity of the primordial images…. Hence, his thinking is of value for his contemporaries only so long as it is manifestly and intelligibly related to the known facts of the time." The 'primordial images' in Adams' mind were those about man, his nature, and particularly the mob mentality, which he believed must be held in check. Jung said, "In pursuit of his ideas, he (this type) is generally stubborn, headstrong, and quite unamenable to influence." Adams himself said he was "puffy, vain, conceited." While not unique to the introverted thinking type, vanity comes with the territory more often than not (in his case, intellect; in other cases, competence, appearance, achievements, etc.); in the end, he admitted vanity was his "cardinal folly." What is important to separate from Adams' type are his unconscious, explosive eruptions and high level of neuroticism (as determined by psychologists Rubenzer and Fascingbauer in their assessment of NEO-PI scores from historians who specialized in Adams).

Jung offers an explanation: "Because he thinks out his problems to the limit, he complicates them and constantly gets tangled in his own scruples and misgivings. However clear to him the inner structure of his thoughts may be, he is not in the least clear where or how they link up with the world of reality. Only with the greatest difficulty will he bring himself to admit that what is clear to him may not be equally clear to everyone." Jung also says, "With the intensification of his type, his convictions become all the more rigid and unbending. His tone becomes personal and surly, and though his ideas may gain in profundity they can no longer be adequately expressed in the material at hand. To compensate for this, he falls back on emotionality and touchiness." And, "Although he will not try to press his convictions on anyone personally, he will burst out with vicious, personal retorts against every criticism, however just." Jung could not have described Adams more clearly had he been his patient at the Burghölzli Clinic in Zurich.

HOW HIS INDEPENDENT LEADERTYPE FORMED

Adams was born in the Massachusetts colony. As a healthy young boy, he loved the outdoors, frequently skipping school to hunt and fish. He said later that he would have preferred a life as a farmer, but his father insisted that he receive a formal education. His father hoped that he might become a clergyman. John attended a dame school, a local school taught by a female teacher that was designed to teach the rudimentary skills of reading and writing. A Latin school, a preparatory school for those who planned to attend college, followed that attendance. Adams entered Harvard at 16, and graduated at just 19. Early on, he was a prolific writer, which would continue throughout his life. He tried teaching, but it became for him "a school of affliction." Jung could have told him why: "...teaching has, at bottom, no interest for him (the introverted thinking type) unless it happens to provide him with a theoretical problem. He is a poor teacher, because all the time he is teaching his thought is occupied with the material itself and not with its presentation."

Children were, at best, an afterthought and at worst, a nuisance, when John was teaching.

But he discovered his forte in the law. He began studying, and in 1770 joined a successful lawyer in Worcester, and in March was chosen to defend the British soldiers involved in the Boston Massacre, where six Boston patriots were shot. Despite being surrounded by adherents to the revolutionary cause, he offered a brilliant defense — another example of both his adherence to principles and his independent spirit. In his closing argument he said, "Facts are stubborn things, and whatever may be our wishes, our inclinations, or dictums of our passions, they cannot alter the state of facts and evidence." (This would be his Take Charge LeaderType talking.) He not only believed the imperial leaders in London had simply blundered; he also suspected that the colonial radicals, including his cousin Samuel Adams, had a hidden agenda, including American independence. He won the case. If his cousin, Sam Adams, and the other revolutionaries were furious with him for defending the soldiers, imagine their disgust at his winning. Consequently, he said "farewell politics," and took a two-and-a-half-year break. (This would have coincided with his midlife turn).

Ultimately, Adams believed that one's principles and their logical conclusion should be sufficient to convince someone. His greatest influence derived from his writings, which took place in his Extraverted Thinking/Take Charge years leading up to his defense of British soldiers. As preparation for his stint in the White House, he was a legislator in the Massachusetts Congress and a delegate to the First and Second Continental Congresses, as well as the Massachusetts Constitutional Convention. He served as commissioner to France, and the first minister (of the United States) to the Netherlands and to England (after the whole Revolutionary War got patched up), and finally vice president of the United States for eight years under George Washington. He served one term, becoming the first president to lose his bid for reelection. So disgusted with the obviously flawed thinking of the electorate, he left the capital before Jefferson's inauguration.

TWO FAMOUS CORRESPONDENCES

Adams exchanged some 300 letters with his wife, Abigail Adams, between 1784 and 1794 when he was serving in the Continental Congress and abroad. He said that Abigail had "always softened and warmed my heart [and] shall polish and refine my sentiments of life and manners," I believe that what little Adams had in the way of a Feeling function, he learned from her and directed towards her. They were supremely devoted to one another. But apart from her, Adams was without any strong friends—and certainly no female friendships. Jung said, "In his personal relations he is taciturn or else throws himself on people who cannot understand him, and for him this is one more proof of the abysmal stupidity of man."

Continuing about the introverted thinking type, he would be seen in "casual acquaintances [as] inconsiderate and domineering. But the better one knows him, the more favorable one's judgment becomes, and his closest friends value his intimacy very highly." For Adams, this would be Abigail, and later in life, Thomas Jefferson. Jung continues about this type: "To outsiders he seems prickly, unapproachable, and arrogant, and sometimes soured as a result of his antisocial prejudices...He becomes more dependent on his intimates."

HOW HIS LEADERTYPE FORMED OVER HIS LIFETIME

- **Independent** – He had an incredibly intense and clearly focused mind. He had unrelenting insistence on legal principle, and objective basis for every argument. He architected the three branches of government, and the upper and lower houses of the Legislative branch.

- **Visionary** – At 20, he shared a very clear vision of an American 'empire' more powerful than the combined force of Europe. He realized everything was subject to change and that he was laying a foundation for centuries to come.

- **Innovating** – He learned from role models how to prosecute best, incorporating the latest techniques, as well as recognizing the 'noble infirmity' that is enthusiasm.

- **Take Charge** – He crusaded against taxation without representation, writing numerous treatises based on legal principles. He began to see success in his practice, and a recognition of his influence. He defended the British soldiers as a matter of principle and to demonstrate the objective rule of law, and he won.

Midlife: After winning the suit, he was ostracized. He says goodbye to politics, and hibernates for almost three years.

- **Inclusive** – He makes his authentic, once-and-for-all commitment to his values of liberty and fairness under the law, authoring many moral indictments of England.

- **Prudent** – He takes office and takes on some of George Washington's dominant type as his vice president for eight years.

- **Proactive** – He becomes president, and while still Independent, his latter life becomes much more active and extraverted. This may be why many perceive John Adams as having an extraverted preference, as it was his emerging LeaderType during his term in office.

- **Persuasive** – Unfortunately, his Persuasive type comes too late to help him in giving due attention to relationships, political parties, consensus, and team building. At the last stage of his life, John Adams follows the promptings of Dr. Benjamin Rush, and extends an olive branch to his one-time arch political foe who had, at one time, also been his vice president, Thomas Jefferson, persuading him with "You know we really shouldn't die without understanding each other."

Adams and Jefferson rekindled their friendship through an amazing correspondence over 15 years until their deaths on the same day, the 50th anniversary of their signing the *Declaration*. In one of those letters Adams makes the case for the influence and impact of his thought leadership:

> "But what do we mean by the American Revolution? Do we mean the American war? The Revolution was effected before the war commenced. The Revolution was in the minds and hearts of the people; a change in their religious sentiments of their duties and obligations....This radical change in the principles, opinions, sentiments, and affections of the people, was the real American Revolution."

John Adams, with his dominant Independent LeaderType, led our nation to independence as its revolutionary-in-chief.

John Adams – Summary Profile

Leadership positions: member, Massachusetts legislature; delegate, First & Second Continental Congresses; member, Provincial Congress of Massachusetts; delegate, Massachusetts Constitutional Convention; commissioner to France; minister to the Netherlands and England; vice-president; president (1797 – 1801)

Age while president: 61 – 65

LeaderTypes:

Strongest: Independent
Supporting: Take Charge
Emerging: Proactive (while president)
Weakest: Persuasive

MBTI preferences (clarity):

* **Introversion** (slight)
* **Intuition** (slight)
* **Thinking** (very clear)
* **Perceiving** (slight)

Prominent Qualities:	Assertive, Achievement striving, Ambitious
Prominent Deficits:	Anger/Hostility, Not modest, Not friendly, Low in moderation, Low in compliance
Motivational need(s):	Achievement, Power
SCARF trigger(s):	Status, Autonomy

CHAPTER TEN

COACHING THE INDEPENDENT
LEADERTYPE IN YOU

If Independent is <u>not</u> your dominant LeaderType, consider these questions for reflection.

- From what perspectives can your present situation be viewed? How would you define it?

- What assumptions are you operating under? How would you categorize your choices?

- What process, expertise and/or logic will you apply to your most challenging problem?

- What are the key variables that, if adjusted, would have an inordinate impact on results?

- How would you impartially describe your team's situation? How can you get more clarity?

- What terms are critical to your team's functioning? Establish what important words mean.

- What criteria can you provide the team to empower them to make decisions and take action?

If Independent is your dominant LeaderType, consider these questions to challenge you.

- When has your autonomy been viewed as an asset? When has it been perceived negatively?

- What subjective or qualitative factors do you need to consider in making the best decision?

- What are your stakeholders' interests? What do your customers need? What's most valued?

- How do you need to communicate and influence the larger audience about your solution?

- When/how might you enter into dialogue/collaboration with an opposing department/group?

- What can you do to build trust, rapport and/or relationship with long-standing adversaries?

- Under what conditions would you be willing to align with popular opinion/group consensus?

QUOTES FOR AN INDEPENDENT JOURNEY

In quiet places, reason abounds. ADLAI E. STEVENSON

Reason is immortal, all else is mortal. PYTHAGORAS

The art of reasoning becomes of first importance.
THOMAS JEFFERSON

Consensus is the negation of leadership. MARGARET THATCHER

Leadership does not always wear the harness of compromise.
WOODROW WILSON

I cannot give you the formula for success, but I can give you the formula for failure which is: Try to please everybody.
HERBERT B. SWOPE

Nothing will ever be attempted if all possible objections must first be overcome. SAMUEL JOHNSON

Chapter Eleven:
Putting All Eight to Work

THIS BOOK HAD A potentially misleading title. You might have expected eight profiles in leadership on eight different leaders, and inferred that one would be your type. And while one of my goals was to help you realize with which president you share the same dominant LeaderType, by now you grasp the more subtle, underlying message: **all eight LeaderTypes are present in The White House — and in you — at any one time.** That's not to say every leader is capable of consciously accessing and using all eight on command, but hopefully she is at least aware of all eight, and perhaps even more importantly, conscious of what she's unconscious of. Unfortunately, this is not always the case — in the White House or in leadership at large. To address this, I believe we need to start developing leaders — and to start earlier — to prepare them for a world which desperately needs self-aware, fully functioning leaders.

Are you more 'awake'? Has your leader awareness increased? Can you see yourself potentially developing all eight of these? That was my intent. As Anthony J. D'Angelo, said, "You can learn a lot from people who view the world differently than you do." The other key take-away, hopefully, is that knowing your personality type can highlight your strengths, biases, and deficiencies in problem-solving, decision-making and leading others.

By exploring these eight examples I sought to show **successful leadership comes in at least eight different varieties**, in four pairs of opposites:

Prudent George Washington ↔ Innovating Franklin Roosevelt

Visionary Thomas Jefferson ↔ Proactive Andrew Jackson

Independent John Adams ↔ Persuasive Harry Truman

Inclusive Abraham Lincoln ↔ Take Charge Theodore Roosevelt

The leaders opposite each other could almost not have been more different personality-wise. They had totally different leadership styles: the ones on the left preferred introversion; the ones on the right, extraversion; the top four focused primarily on how they perceived their world; the bottom four, mostly on their judgments of the world; some focused on details, others context; four decided primarily with their head, four mostly with their heart — all due to their personality type, and all critical to leadership.

My second conclusion is that most of **these leaders demonstrated all eight LeaderTypes,** and thus practiced eight perspectives in viewing world affairs. As divergent, complex, and changing as our world is, leaders need perspective-taking almost as much as they need agility. Leaders need to realize that their way of seeing the world, understanding an issue, or making a decision is just that, their way—not the only way. Leaders need to realize that there are seven other ways of looking at every challenge, and that seeking multiple perspectives is not a weakness. It is a strength.

Unfortunately, the reason perspective-seeking is needed is that not all people—or leaders—develop all eight within themselves. In fact, some have barely one differentiated LeaderType to inform them. They operate largely out of their unconscious, and are easily triggered. This makes for a very unbalanced, immature, one-dimensional leader (e.g., all extraverted with no reflection, introspection, or deliberation). These one-style-fits-all leaders usually expect the world—and their followers—to adjust to them, resulting in egocentric biases and/or narcissistic behaviors.

My third point is **all leaders need balance**. The truly great leaders are those who evolve. They know who they are, they develop what they can become, and ironically, they deconstruct their ego at midlife—achieving 'twice born' status. The result is an even better (because it's more whole) version of their leader-self—from incorporating all those LeaderTypes previously dismissed as 'not me.' This is an essential truth every person older than 40 understands, and Jung surmised: "We cannot live the afternoon of life according to the program of life's morning; for what was great in the morning will be little at evening, and what in the morning was true will at evening have become a lie."

Fourth, **leaders must develop intentionally**. Jung again: "Personality can never develop unless the individual chooses his own way, consciously." Think of the eight as 'the cards you were dealt' at birth, and further imagine those cards are face down. Jung's theory is that you are innately predisposed to favor certain cards in your deck. Spoto says there's an order in which you will turn them over. But as Jung said, "A tree must grow in the soil in which it is planted." If the 'soil' in which you are planted is conducive to your predisposed nature (i.e., your parents honor your type preferences, and nurture your unique self-expression) then you have a better chance to grow according to the sequence Spoto describes. If, however, the challenges you need to grow don't manifest themselves, and you're not intentional about developing yourself as a leader, and you don't plumb and embrace the unconscious rumblings that percolate up in your individuation process, then you won't blossom into a fully conscious carrier of all eight cards—much less be able to play the right card when life presents itself.

> *Amazingly few people know how they get things done. Indeed, most of us do not even know that different people work and perform differently. Too many people work in ways that are not their ways, and that almost guarantees non-performance.*
> PETER DRUCKER

If, on the other hand, you pay attention, and are intentional in 'playing' your cards then you will achieve eight ways of dealing with your world, and I submit, you will have lived a full life. You will have gained eight forms of consciousness, eight perspectives with which to understand situations, and eight ways of leading. You will be, in effect, a whole person. And that really is the goal: not to be perfect, but whole. That you embrace not only the parts of you that your ego identifies as 'me,' but you also embrace the 'not me' within you, and incorporate those, becoming who you really are.

Finally, **no type is best, and every type is best.** This is the answer I have been seeking for twelve years, ever since an emerging leader-student in one of my workshops posed the question: What type leader is the best? I now have the answer: "Yours is." Strive to be the best version of yourself, and you'll take a giant leap toward authenticity. Don't imitate some random leader. In the words of Herman Hesse, "It is not our purpose to become each other; it is to recognize each other, to learn to see the other and honor him for what he is." If you're going to read a biography, read one of a leader that shares your LeaderType (or the one you're currently cultivating). Being yourself doesn't mean excusing your style as 'just the way you are.' Each LeaderType comes with its own peculiar strengths and weaknesses. It's not enough just to be authentic, a leader must be effective: you need to own your stuff. Embrace your brand, but don't stop there: leverage your natural strengths and mitigate your just-as-natural weaknesses. Know yourself. Be yourself. Coach yourself.

> *Insist on yourself; never imitate. Your own gift you can present every moment with the cumulative force of a whole life's cultivation; but of the adopted talent of another you have only an extemporaneous half-possession.* RALPH WALDO EMERSON

My other answer to that student is "It depends." That 'best' is the one best-suited to a given situation. In his book, *Energies and Patterns in Psychological Type,* John Beebe says, "…development of consciousness involves the ability to summon the various functions at appropriate times in appropriate ways." Can you call forth the LeaderType(s) most needed or relevant when presented with a challenge?

Realizing that's not always possible, the next best thing is to contribute your best to a team or organization. One specific way, as an example, is how each LeaderType contributes a unique perspective to the strategic planning process.

- **Prudent** leaders know how we got where we are, can assess the group's mission-relevant strengths and weaknesses, and often caution against known risks.

- **Proactive** leaders grasp an awareness of the current situation, identifying the most pressing threats and opportunities, stressing immediate action on any 'quick wins.'

- **Innovating** leaders offer scenarios of how the group's world might evolve, 'connecting the dots' to apprehend what parts of the organization need to be transformed — and how.

- **Visionary** leaders see how the end game will play out, and working backward from that, craft a roadmap to take the organization forward, anticipating issues and challenges.

- **Inclusive** leaders realize what will matter most on the journey: what values must be shared and protected so we stay true to who we are, both internally and externally.

- **Persuasive** leaders align the organizational culture with the strategy, knowing who needs to be influenced — and how — in terms of employees, stakeholders, partners and customers.

- **Take Charge** leaders set stretch goals, develop plans to implement the strategy, clarify roles, responsibilities and ownership in order to make things happen, and hold people accountable.

- **Independent** leaders provide a sanity check on the overall process, put in place a balanced scorecard to measure progress, and establish criteria for smart, empowered decision-making.

If one of these LeaderTypes does not have a seat at the table, I predict that aspect of your organization's strategic planning will suffer. Peter Drucker said, "An organization cannot overcome all weaknesses, but it can make them irrelevant. Its task is to use the strength of each individual as a building block for joint performance." It really does take a village — unless you have an enlightened, fully aware and wholly functioning adult at the helm (which is doubtful).

Consider the global village we inhabit. These eight ways of seeing the world are universal — they exist in every tribe, nation and culture — and in every person in those communities. We often insist that one or a few of the eight are 'us' and the others are 'not us.' Perhaps Jung has an answer for that too: "If a worldwide consciousness could arise that all division and all antagonism are due to the splitting of opposites in the psyche, then one would really know where to attack." In case you missed it, he means within you. The problems we perceive to be with 'them' are actually unconscious perspectives within us. The challenge for warring tribes within organizations is the same for individuals: through a collaborative process, to mutually respect differences, hold the tension of opposite perspectives, and somehow transcend them in discerning a new way forward. The path of personal individuation (becoming whole) says work on yourself. Recognize and embrace the opposites within you. Collaborate within your Self.

The real message of this book can be found on the front cover, not in the title or subtitle, but at the center of the mock presidential seal: ***E pluribus unum.*** **Out of many, one.** Once the de facto motto of the United States, it reminded early citizens of whence they came, and the incredible significance of 13 diverse, disjointed colonies coming together to form one nation. That is your challenge. Out of the eight LeaderTypes in *your* house, what will become the authentic synthesis of your leader-self? How will you resist the urge to project the ones you label 'not me' onto 'them,' essentially turning invisible, internal nemeses into externally scapegoated enemies? How will you lead yourself through that internal conflict? May I suggest you begin by reflecting on your leadership more deliberately, and more often? And that you consider all your LeaderTypes — including your lesser developed ones — and thus, own all of you. *E pluribus unum.*

We always think we are at the end of our discoveries. We never are. We go on discovering that we are this, that, and other things, and sometimes we have astounding experiences. CARL JUNG

Finally, I wish you challenges that grow your leadership. Move into them. Trust the process. Find your true leader-self—that all-encompassing, highly functioning leader within you—in those challenges. And once you think you've arrived, break that self-image, and rebuild another. I think it will make for a much more interesting journey, and make you a much better leader.

About the Author

CASH KEAHEY IS BOTH a teacher and student of leaders and leadership. He learned first-hand about political influence at an early age when a neighbor in the grocery store announced he was voting for Cash's dad for school board because of his upstanding conduct. ("I was like Harry Truman as a kid," says Cash.) He would eventually help his father campaign for state office. After earning a bachelor's in marketing, Keahey went to work in computer hardware sales—influencing others. He later got his MBA from the University of Houston.

A 23-year professional career inside global Fortune 500s in diverse functions and industries exposed Cash to different corporate cultures with different styles of leadership. His first management job was to lead the development of marketing programs, which paved the way to managing a sales territory, and subsequent position of leadership directing an enterprise-wide culture change. Through these experiences, Keahey realized the symbiotic relationship between leadership and culture: that leaders create a culture around them, but in order to succeed, must lead in a culture that values their uniqueness.

Cash now uses his natural gift of engaging audiences to facilitate workshops and speak to leaders around the world. Since being qualified in the Myers-Briggs Type

Indicator® (MBTI) in 1999, he has deepened his knowledge of Jungian psychology to become a leader in the type community. From Jung's theory of psychological types, Cash developed eight LeaderType™ profiles. This book is a culmination of twelve years of research into eight 'great' or 'near great' leader-presidents, revealing how their personality types shaped this country. Cash's predominant LeaderTypes are Proactive, Persuasive, and Inclusive.

Appendices

1. THE PERSONALITY DATABASE OF THE PRESIDENTS

THE MOST SIGNIFICANT BASIS for my hypothesis of each president's dominant LeaderType comes from a database developed by the authors of *Personality, Character and Leadership in the White House: Psychologists Assess the Presidents*. Steven J. Rubenzer and Thomas R. Faschingbauer recruited 120 generalists and experts on certain presidencies to complete a psychological inventory, the 240-item Revised NEO-PI, on 42 presidents. (Neither President Barak Obama nor Donald Trump were included in this analysis.) The *NEO* Personality Inventory measures the 'Big Five' factors of personality, each factor having six facets. The factors are Neuroticism, Extroversion, Openness, Agreeableness, and Conscientiousness, sometimes referred to as the Five Factor Model (Note: The authors' surveys of presidential character and success were not included in my analysis. Interestingly, they found no correlation between character and success in the U.S. presidency.)

The 120 raters fell into two categories: specialists on a particular president or era, and generalists having broad, comparative knowledge about all of them. For the eight presidents profiled in this book, between 13 to 20 raters (see table below) completed the Revised NEO-PI, and their results were averaged. One significant benefit of this process is a reduction of individual historian bias. A biography of a leader is just one person's subjective view of that president's life and life's work. Averaging multiple perspectives with a standardized, widely accepted tool provides a credible base for analysis. This table shows the number of expert raters, both historian-specialists and historian-generalists, and the total number of raters for each president profiled in this book.

President	Specialist Raters	Generalist Raters	Total Raters
Washington	10	7	17
J. Adams	6	7	13
Jefferson	11	7	18
Jackson	7	7	14
Lincoln	8	7	15
T. Roosevelt	7	7	14
F. Roosevelt	13	7	20
Truman	7	7	14

NOTE: That the same seven generalists rated all eight presidents means those raters brought a common standard to their item responses.

2. THE RATIONALE FOR THESE EIGHT PRESIDENTS

In selecting these eight presidents to study I relied on older rankings of the presidents (to avoid recent politicization of presidential rankings), primarily those of Arthur Schlesinger, Sr., Siena Research Institute, Robert Murray and Tim Blessing. The Murray-Blessing study (1982) was one of the few, to my knowledge, that asked historians evaluating the presidents to self-identify as either conservative or liberal. Here are their two lists:

Rank	Conservatives (n = 50)	Liberals (n = 190)
1	Abraham Lincoln	Franklin Roosevelt
2	George Washington	Abraham Lincoln
3	Franklin Roosevelt	George Washington
4	Thomas Jefferson	Thomas Jefferson
5	Theodore Roosevelt	Theodore Roosevelt
6	Andrew Jackson	Woodrow Wilson
7	Harry Truman	Andrew Jackson
8	Woodrow Wilson	Harry Truman
9	Dwight Eisenhower	Lyndon Johnson
10	John Adams	John Adams

The fact that two hundred forty historians surveyed reached consensus on nine of the top ten presidents is significant. The only differences between the two lists: Liberals included LBJ in the top ten, while conservatives included Eisenhower. More fascinating to me, of course, is that among the nine that appeared on both are eight different dominant LeaderTypes.

3. TRANSLATING NEO-PI RESULTS INTO TYPE PREFERENCES AND LEADERTYPES

To hypothesize each president's Myers-Briggs type, it was first necessary to establish what relationship (if any) exists between NEO facets (within the five factors) and MBTI dichotomies. The database received from Rubenzer and Faschingbauer had averaged results at the facet level for 42 presidents. For each facet there are eight items on the questionnaire. Each item was analyzed in terms of its expressing a MBTI preference (E – I, S – N, T – F, J – P) or a Jungian polarity (e.g., Introverted Sensation vs. Extraverted Intuition). Even where labels were similar (e.g., Extraversion vs. Extroversion), care was taken to clarify differences. One facet of the trait Extroversion (in the Big Five) is Positive Emotions. That trait is characterized by demonstrating joy or happiness, which is not part of Jung's view of extraversion; therefore, that facet was not included in determining a preference for Extraversion in Jungian terms.

If four or more items within a facet reflected a preference or polarity, then it was included in the calculation of that type preference or LeaderType. Between three to four facets were used to calculate MBTI dichotomy scores, and between four to five facets were used to calculate LeaderType scores. In most cases, the facets were equally weighted; however, when, for example, only 4 out of 8 items reflected that preference or type versus another facet where all 8 items reflected a particular preference/ type, the latter was weighted heavier in the algorithm used to calculate MBTI results and LeaderTypes.

Despite considerable differences at the facet and item levels, I found strong correlations between my calculated Myers-Briggs preference scores for the 42 Presidents, and the Big Five factor scores for that population:

MBTI preference	Big Five	Correlation coefficient
Extraversion – Introversion	Extroversion	.86
Intuition – Sensation	Openness	.92
Feeling – Thinking	Agreeableness	.94
Judging – Perceiving	Conscientiousness	.88

Notwithstanding the different philosophical basis of each system (behaviors are caused by traits versus behaviors are an expression of type), the high correlation suggests perhaps a distinction without (much of) a difference.

An algorithm based on this analysis was then developed to indicate each president's Myers-Briggs type preferences. Applying that algorithm to the data yielded extremes on both ends of each dichotomy. For example, Theodore Roosevelt's result represented the Extraversion end of the E – I dichotomy, and Calvin Coolidge's the extreme for Introversion. To find 'the middle' on which to sort, for example, those with an extraverted preference from those with an introverted one, I reviewed statistical breakdowns of the dichotomies among U.S. males, and studied individual presidents' tendencies from biographies and historical information. I then established 'degrees of confidence' in my hypothesis with a term familiar to anyone who has ever received a report of their indicated type results: preference clarity. For all 42 Presidents for all dichotomies I established a slight, moderate, clear and very clear preference. This effectively translates into a confidence level about each president's type: slight, moderate, strong or very strong.

4. MBTI DICHOTOMIES AND PRESIDENTS WITH THE CLEAREST PREFERENCES

Here are the Presidents with clearest preferences for each of the four dichotomies. (If unfamiliar with the Myers-Briggs typology, read the headings of each section for a preliminary sort of your preferences.)

Extraversion – Directing one's energy outward to the external world of people, events or things. Energized by initiating contact or interacting with one's outer world.	**Introversion** – Directing one's energy and attention inward to your own ideas, thoughts, values, memories or hunches. Energized by processing information or choices internally.
Theodore Roosevelt	Calvin Coolidge
Andrew Jackson	James Madison
Lyndon Johnson	Grover Cleveland
Bill Clinton	John Q. Adams
John Kennedy	James Monroe
Warren Harding	Herbert Hoover
Harry Truman	Benjamin Harrison
Franklin Roosevelt	James Buchanan

NOTE: The first six presidents of the United States had an introverted preference. It wasn't until Andrew Jackson that a president with clear preference for extraversion led this country.

Sensation – Paying attention to tangible, sensed information. Valuing data, specifics or details about the present and/or known information established from past experience.	**Intuition** – Paying attention to possibilities — especially about the future. Focusing on intangibles, and the meaning and interconnectedness of everything everywhere.
George W. Bush	Thomas Jefferson
William Howard Taft	John Kennedy
James Buchanan	John Q. Adams
William McKinley	Abraham Lincoln
Herbert Hoover	Theodore Roosevelt
Harry Truman	James Garfield
Andrew Jackson	Bill Clinton

Thinking – Reaching a conclusion using impartial criteria (e.g., principles). Defining categories or clarifying situations using logic. Analyzing impacts based on cause-and-effect, or pros-and-cons. Being tough-minded.	**Feeling** – Reaching a conclusion based on personal values or group norms. Realizing who and what matters most. Harmonizing a decision around people's needs, interests or concerns. Being tender-hearted.
Richard Nixon	Rutherford Hayes
John Adams	Warren Harding
Andrew Jackson	Abraham Lincoln
Andrew Johnson	Jimmy Carter
Lyndon Johnson	William McKinley
John Q. Adams	Bill Clinton
George W. Bush	Millard Fillmore
James Polk	James Monroe

Judging – Having a structured, methodical approach to one's outer world. Liking things organized and planned in advance. Wanting to be prepared to avoid any last-minute stress.	**Perceiving** – Having a spontaneous, flexible approach to one's outer world. Letting plans emerge. Keeping things open-ended. Adapting to or improvising with whatever unfolds.
Jimmy Carter	Bill Clinton
Woodrow Wilson	Ulysses Grant
George Washington	George W. Bush
Herbert Hoover	George H. W. Bush

Dwight Eisenhower	John Kennedy
Theodore Roosevelt	Warren Harding
Richard Nixon	Andrew Jackson
Rutherford Hayes	Ronald Reagan
James Buchanan	Abraham Lincoln

5. TYPING THE PRESIDENTS: MYERS-BRIGGS TYPE TABLE AND DOMINANT LEADERTYPES

The number of U.S. presidents of each MBTI type reveals the diversity of personality types that have occupied the White House. Here is the type table for the 42 Presidents in my database:

ISTJ	ISFJ	INFJ	INTJ
8	4	3	1
ISTP	ISFP	INFP	INTP
3	2	2	2
ESTP	ESFP	ENFP	ENTP
2	1	6	2
ESTJ	ESFJ	ENFJ	ENTJ
3	2	0	1

The following lists the 42 presidents, by dominant LeaderType and supporting LeaderType, chronologically:

Dominant LeaderType

- **Supporting LeaderType:** President(s)

Prudent

- **Take Charge** Washington, Buchanan, Cleveland, Wilson, Coolidge, Hoover, Eisenhower, Nixon
- **Persuasive** Madison, Fillmore, B. Harrison, McKinley

Visionary

- **Persuasive** Jefferson, Hayes, Carter
- **Take Charge** Van Buren

Inclusive

- **Proactive** Monroe, Grant
- **Innovating** Lincoln, Garfield

Independent

- **Proactive** Polk, Taft, G. H. W. Bush
- **Innovating** J. Adams, J. Q. Adams

Proactive

- **Independent** Jackson, G. W. Bush
- **Inclusive** Pierce

Innovating

- **Inclusive**   W. H. Harrison, Harding, F. Roosevelt, Kennedy, Reagan, Clinton
- **Independent** Tyler, Arthur

Persuasive

- **Prudent**   Truman, Ford
- **Visionary**   (none)

Take Charge

- **Prudent**   Taylor, A. Johnson, L. Johnson
- **Visionary**   T. Roosevelt

6. DEGREE OF EACH LEADERTYPE IN THESE EIGHT PRESIDENTS

A separate algorithm was developed to indicate the degree of each LeaderType in each president. Comparing an individual president's results to the database of 42, a percentile rank was generated for the eight presidents. This could be considered a proxy for the relative 'strength' of the LeaderType within that president. For each president, their profiled LeaderType was the strongest, relatively speaking, in their 'portfolio' (columns). And, in three out of eight cases, that particular president's LeaderType was the strongest of all 42 presidents (100%). The bold percentile is the president's greatest strength in terms of LeaderType. Except for Truman's Persuasive LeaderType (which ranks third among this group), the other presidents' LeaderTypes are the strongest (or best representations) of that LeaderType among this population.

Percentile Rank of each LeaderType
Represented in the 8 Presidents

	Washington	Jackson	FDR	Jefferson	Lincoln	Truman	T. Roosevelt	Adams
Prudent	**95%**	7%	20%	34%	51%	61%	39%	29%
Proactive	22%	**100%**	85%	32%	66%	73%	93%	63%
Innovating	20%	59%	**93%**	63%	88%	22%	95%	32%
Visionary	61%	2%	56%	**100%**	93%	5%	71%	34%
Inclusive	27%	2%	68%	88%	**98%**	39%	5%	10%
Persuasive	27%	7%	83%	71%	95%	**76%**	71%	2%
Take Charge	93%	95%	51%	32%	46%	63%	**98%**	76%
Independent	61%	63%	37%	71%	24%	5%	34%	100%

n = 42

My results support recent research by Mark Majors PhD and Ray Moody PhD, using the MajorsPTI® (Personality Type Indicator) to measure the eight types. Their findings, using different approaches on two large samples (n = 9,972 and n = 5,247), confirm Jung's theory: everyone has all eight types.

7. SEQUENCE OF TYPE DEVELOPMENT – ANGELO SPOTO MODEL

Angelo Spoto, Jungian psychotherapist and author of *Jung's Typology in Perspective*, hypothesizes that individuals come into greater awareness of all eight function-attitudes *(LeaderTypes)* in a particular order based on their type (e.g., 'best fit' MBTI). My research correlates with Spoto's model, which suggests that typological development has a specific pattern that is born out in this study.

ISTJ	ISFJ	ISTP	INTP	ISFP	INFP	INTJ	INFJ
Prudent	Prudent	Independent	Independent	Inclusive	Inclusive	Visionary	Visionary
Independent	Inclusive	Prudent	Visionary	Prudent	Visionary	Independent	Inclusive
Take Charge	Persuasive	Proactive	Innovating	Proactive	Innovating	Take Charge	Persuasive
Proactive	Proactive	Take Charge	Take Charge	Persuasive	Persuasive	Innovating	Innovating
MID–LIFE							
Visionary	Visionary	Inclusive	Inclusive	Independent	Independent	Prudent	Prudent
Inclusive	Independent	Visionary	Prudent	Visionary	Prudent	Inclusive	Independent
Persuasive	Take Charge	Innovating	Proactive	Innovating	Proactive	Persuasive	Take Charge
Innovating	Innovating	Persuasive	Persuasive	Take Charge	Take Charge	Proactive	Proactive

ENFP	ENTP	ENFJ	ESFJ	ENTJ	ESTJ	ESFP	ESTP
Innovating	Innovating	Persuasive	Persuasive	Take Charge	Take Charge	Proactive	Proactive
Persuasive	Take Charge	Innovating	Proactive	Innovating	Proactive	Persuasive	Take Charge
Inclusive	Independent	Visionary	Prudent	Visionary	Prudent	Inclusive	Independent
Visionary	Visionary	Inclusive	Inclusive	Independent	Independent	Prudent	Prudent
MID–LIFE							
Proactive	Proactive	Take Charge	Take Charge	Persuasive	Persuasive	Innovating	Innovating
Take Charge	Persuasive	Proactive	Innovating	Proactive	Innovating	Take Charge	Persuasive
Independent	Inclusive	Prudent	Visionary	Prudent	Visionary	Independent	Inclusive
Prudent	Prudent	Independent	Independent	Inclusive	Inclusive	Visionary	Visionary

Spoto's model additionally has a tie to what Jungians refer to as "the problem of opposites." Briefly, there is always a tension of opposites operating in the psyche that serves to dynamically and creatively move the individuation process along. Individuation in Jungian psychology refers to the innate drive for wholeness in any given personality. In typological terms, this creative tension of opposites is what moves the developmental line along. I have chosen not to focus on that aspect of Spoto's work. I have, however, found that the developmental line he has proposed from a typological perspective has great explanatory power when examining the development of the leadership style of presidents. My research into LeaderTypes in effect supports Spoto's model.

Bibliography

Throughout entire text:

Personality, Character & Leadership in the White House: Psychologists Assess the Presidents. Rubenzer, Steven J. & Faschingbauer, Thomas R. Brassey's. (2004)

The Presidential Character: Predicting Performance in the White House. Barber, James David. Fourth Edition. Prentice Hall. (1992)

The Presidents. Beschloss, Michael, general editor. American Heritage Inc. (2003)

Presidential Courage: Brave Leaders and How They Changed America 1789 – 1989. Beschloss, Michael. Simon & Schuster. (2007)

Presidential Leadership: Rating the Best and the Worst in the White House. Taranto, James & Leo, Leonard. Free Press. (2005)

Presidential Temperament. Choiniere, Ray & Keirsey, David. Prometheus Nemesis Book Company. (1992)

The Power of the Modern Presidency. Hargrove, Edwin C. Alfred A. Knopf. (1974)

The Founding Fathers on Leadership: Classic Teamwork in Changing Times. Phillips, Donald T. Warner Books, Inc. (1997)

Psychological Types. Jung, C. G. Originally published in German by Rascher Verlag in Zurich (1921); Bollingen Series XX. Princeton University Press. (1971)

Gifts Differing: Understanding Personality Type. Briggs Myers, Isabel with Myers, Peter B. Davies-Black Publishing. (1995)

Jung's Typology in Perspective: revised edition. Spoto, Angelo. Chiron Publications. (1999)

Energies and Patterns in Psychological Type: The Reservoir of Consciousness. Beebe, John. Routledge. (2017)

Introduction to Type and Leadership. Richmond, Sharon Leibowitz. CPP Inc. (2008)

Introduction to Type and Emotional Intelligence. Pearman, Roger R. CPP Inc. (2002)

Introduction to Type and Coaching. Hirsh, Sandra Krebs & Kise, Jane A. G. CPP Inc. (2011)

8 Keys to Self-leadership: From Awareness to Action. Nardi, Dario. Unite Business Press. (2005)

The Neuroscience of Personality: Brain-savvy Insights for All Types of People. Nardi, Dario. Radiance House. (2011)

Coaching with the Brain in Mind: Foundations for Practice. Rock, David & Page, Linda J. John Wiley & Sons, Inc. (2009)

The Achieving Society. McClelland, David C. D. Van Nostrand Company, Inc. (1961)

https://news.cebglobal.com/press-releases?item=67148

https://en.wikipedia.org/wiki/
Historical_rankings_of_presidents_of_the_United_States

http://greenpeakpartners.com/uploads/Green-Peak_
Cornell-University-Study_What-predicts-success.pdf

Chapter 3, George Washington

George Washington: In His Own Words. Harrison,
Maureen & Gilbert, Steve, Editors. Excellent Books.
(1997)

Washington: The Indispensable Man. Flexner, James
Thomas. Little, Brown and Company. (1984)

The First of Men: A Life of George Washington. Ferling,
John E. University of Tennessee Press. (1988)

Chapter 4, Andrew Jackson

Andrew Jackson: His Life and Times. Brands, H. W.
Anchor Books, a division of Random House, Inc. (2005)

Chapter 5, Franklin D. Roosevelt

Franklin D. Roosevelt: A Rendezvous with Destiny. Freidel,
Frank. Little, Brown and Company. (1990)

Nothing to Fear: Lessons in Leadership from FDR. Axelrod,
Alan. Penguin Books Ltd. (2003)

Chapter 6, Thomas Jefferson

American Sphinx: The Character of Thomas Jefferson. Ellis,
Joseph J. Knopf. (1997)

The Inner Jefferson: Portrait of a Grieving Optimist. Burstein, Andrew. University Press of Virginia. (1995)

The Lost World of Thomas Jefferson. Boorstin, Daniel J. The University of Chicago Press. (1948)

The Process of Government under Jefferson. Cunningham, Noble E. Princeton University Press. (1978)

Thomas Jefferson: An Intimate History. Brodie, Fawn M. Norton. (1974)

Understanding Thomas Jefferson. Halliday, E. M. HarperCollins Publishers Inc. (2001)

Chapter 7, Abraham Lincoln

Team of Rivals: The Political Genius of Abraham Lincoln. Goodwin, Doris Kearns. Simon & Schuster, Inc. (2005)

Lincoln on Leadership. Phillips, Donald T. Warner Books, Inc. (1992)

Abraham Lincoln: The Man Behind the Myths. Oates, Stephen B. Harper & Row Publishers. (1984)

Chapter 8, Harry Truman

Harry S. Truman in His Own Words. Hillman, William. Bonanza Books. (1984)

The Buck Stops Here: The Words of Harry S. Truman. Donovan, Robert J. Newmarket Press. (1984)

Truman. McCullough, David. Simon & Schuster, Inc. (1992)

Where the Buck Stops: The Personal and Private Writings of Harry S. Truman. Truman, Margaret. Warner Books. (1982)

Chapter 9, Theodore Roosevelt

Theodore Roosevelt: A Life. Miller, Nathan. HarperCollins Publishers Inc. (1992)

Theodore Roosevelt, CEO: 7 Principles to Guide and Inspire Modern Leaders. Axelrod, Alan. Sterling Publishing Co., Inc. (2012)

Chapter 10, John Adams

John Adams: A Life. Ferling, John. Henry Holt and Company, Inc. (1992)

John Adams. McCullough, David. Simon & Schuster, Inc. (2001)

John Adams: Party of One. Grant, James. Farrar, Straus and Giroux (2005)

The Adams Papers. www.masshist.org